Thank you for purchasing "The Still and Quiet Life"

Grayscale coloring is a wonderful art genre that has become popular with colorist like you. Skip the stages of design, perspective plotting, and value studies. Go straight to what you love the most - COLOR!! Whether you choose realistic or stylistic - each design can become your own unique color expression.

Search YouTube for grayscale coloring tutorials or use your browser to search the many websites with tips and instructions on this art form, as well as suggestions for types and brand choices of colored pencils, pens and markers.

Credit for the original designs in this book goes to the many artists who contribute their fine work to the galleries of pixabay.com.

Thank you for purchasing this edition. Please look for other coloring books by author/illustrator Patricia Markham.

If you are pleased with your purchase, please take a moment right now, while it is in your hand and on your mind, to leave a positive review and a "5-star" rating on amazon.com. It will encourage the production of more of these beautiful adult coloring books. Your comments are sincerely appreciated.

Try your colors here.
If you are using pens or markers, it is a good idea to place a blotter or scrap sheet of paper underneath the design you are working on to protect the design behind it. Enjoy!

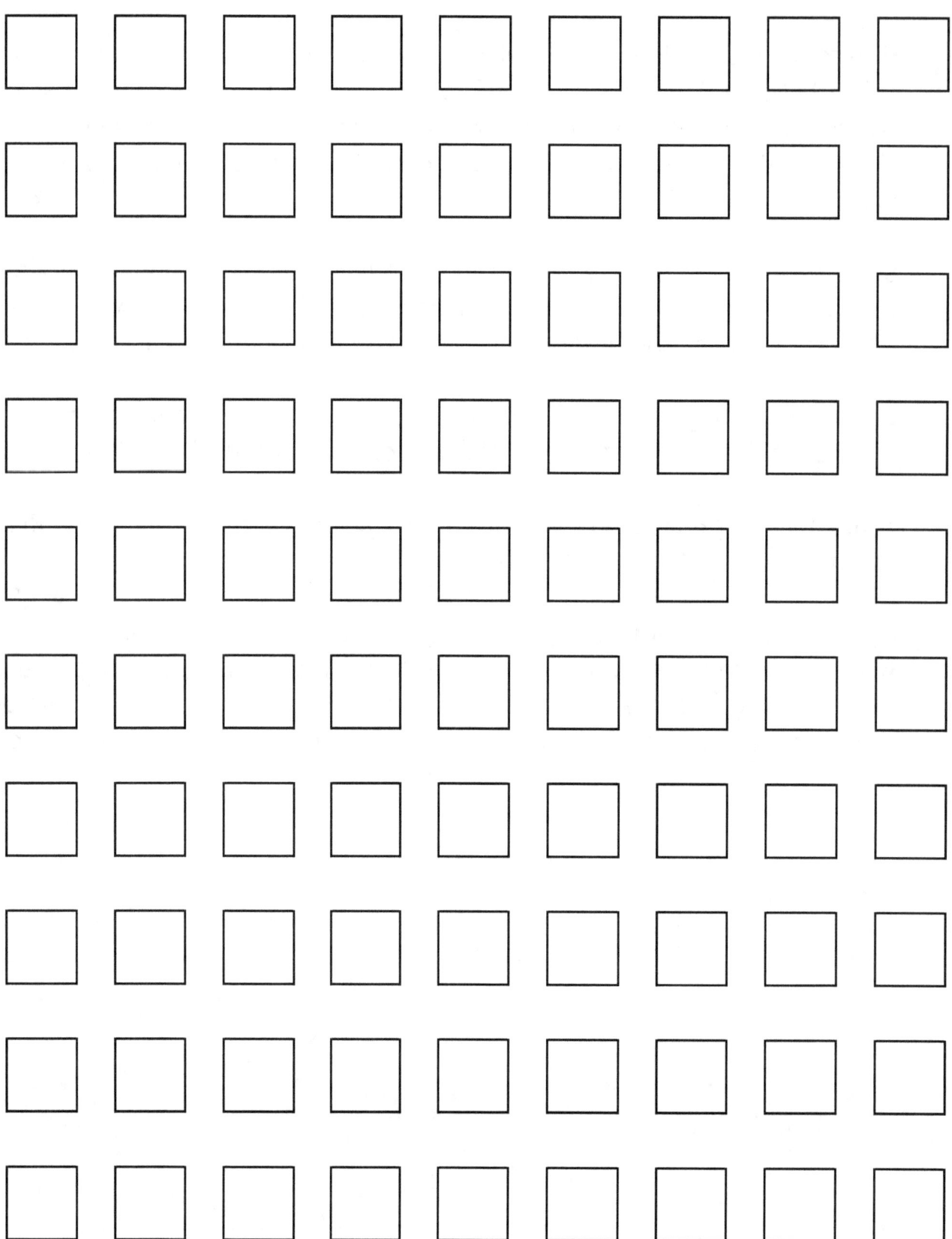

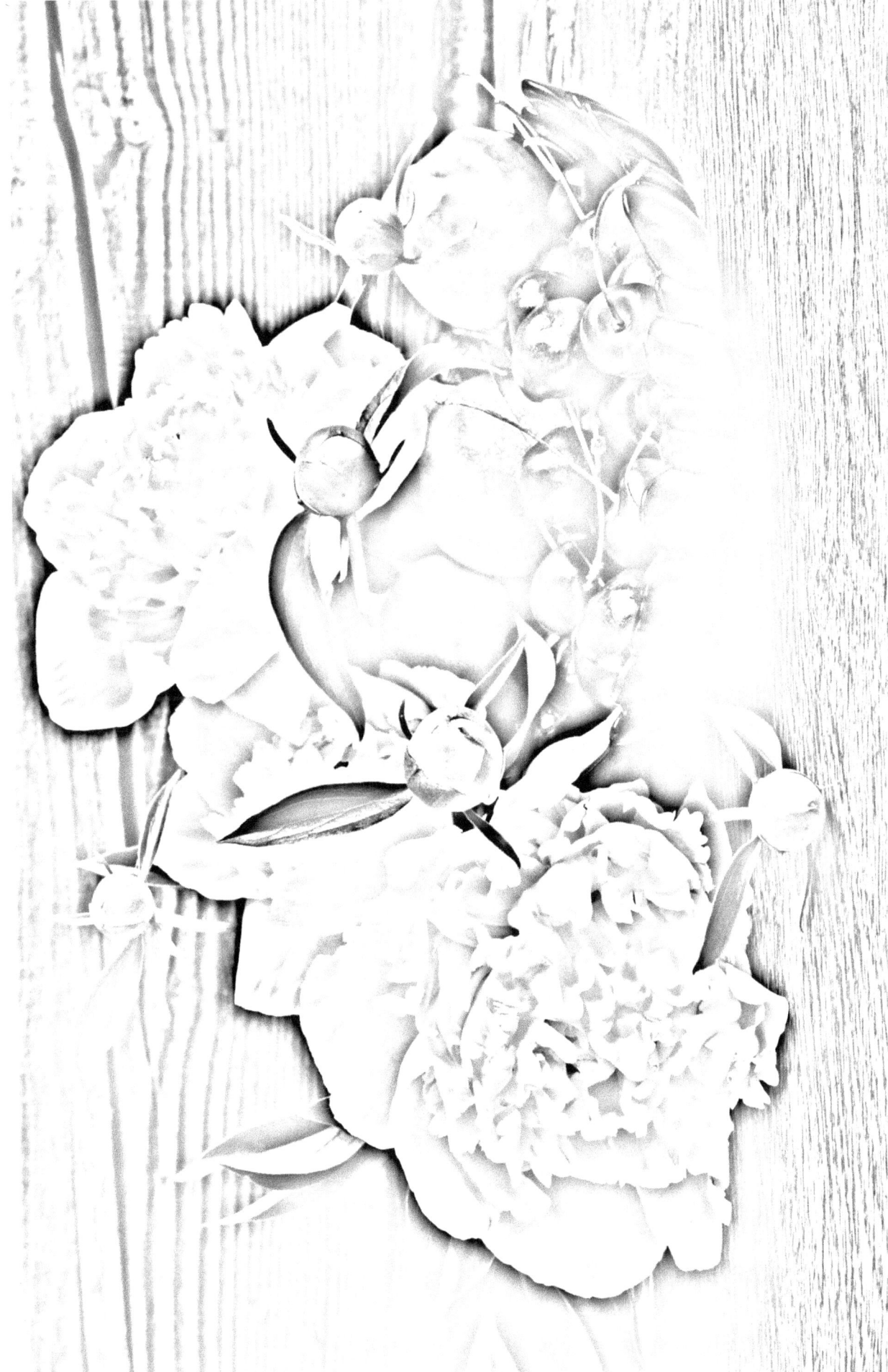

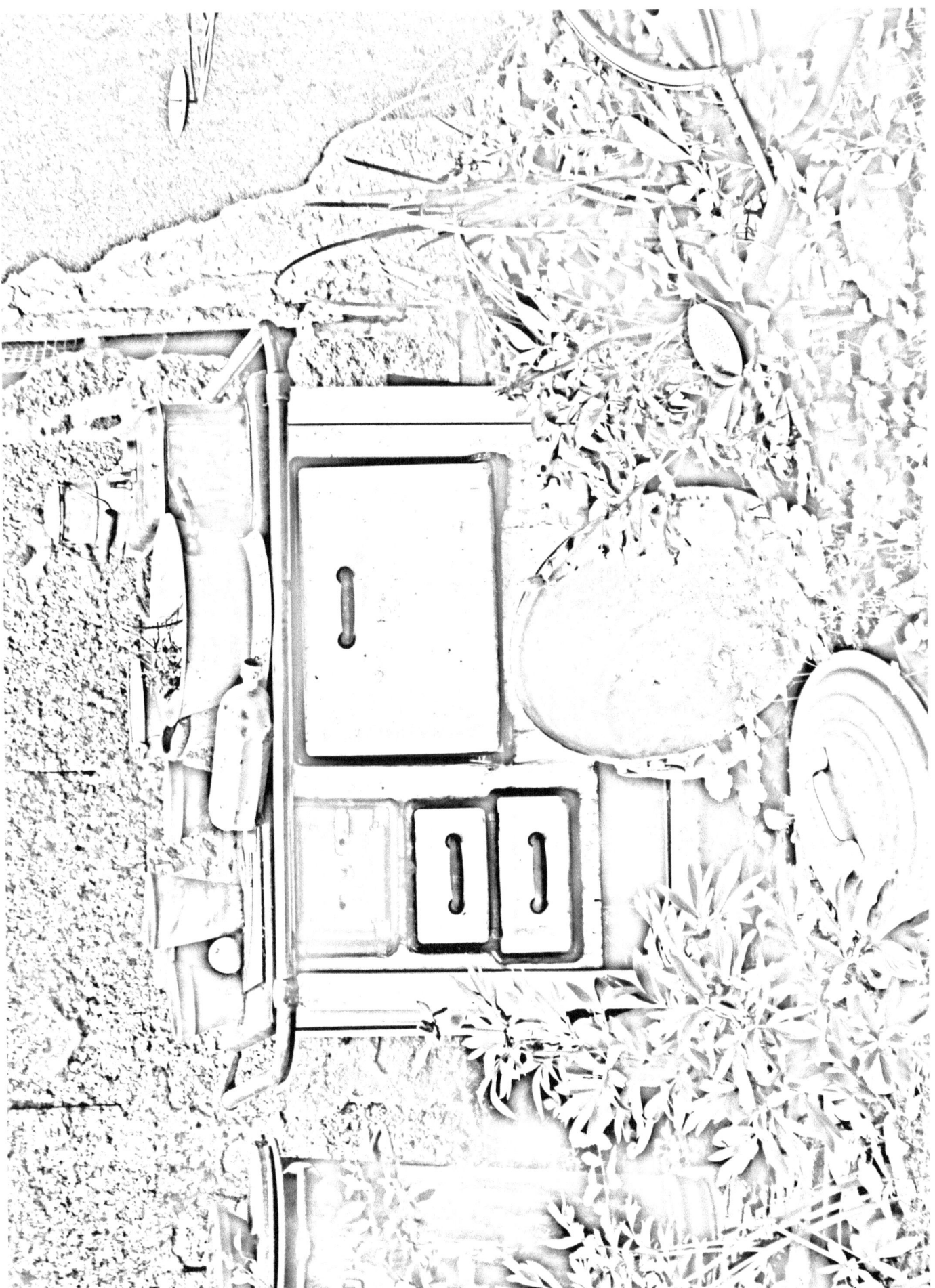

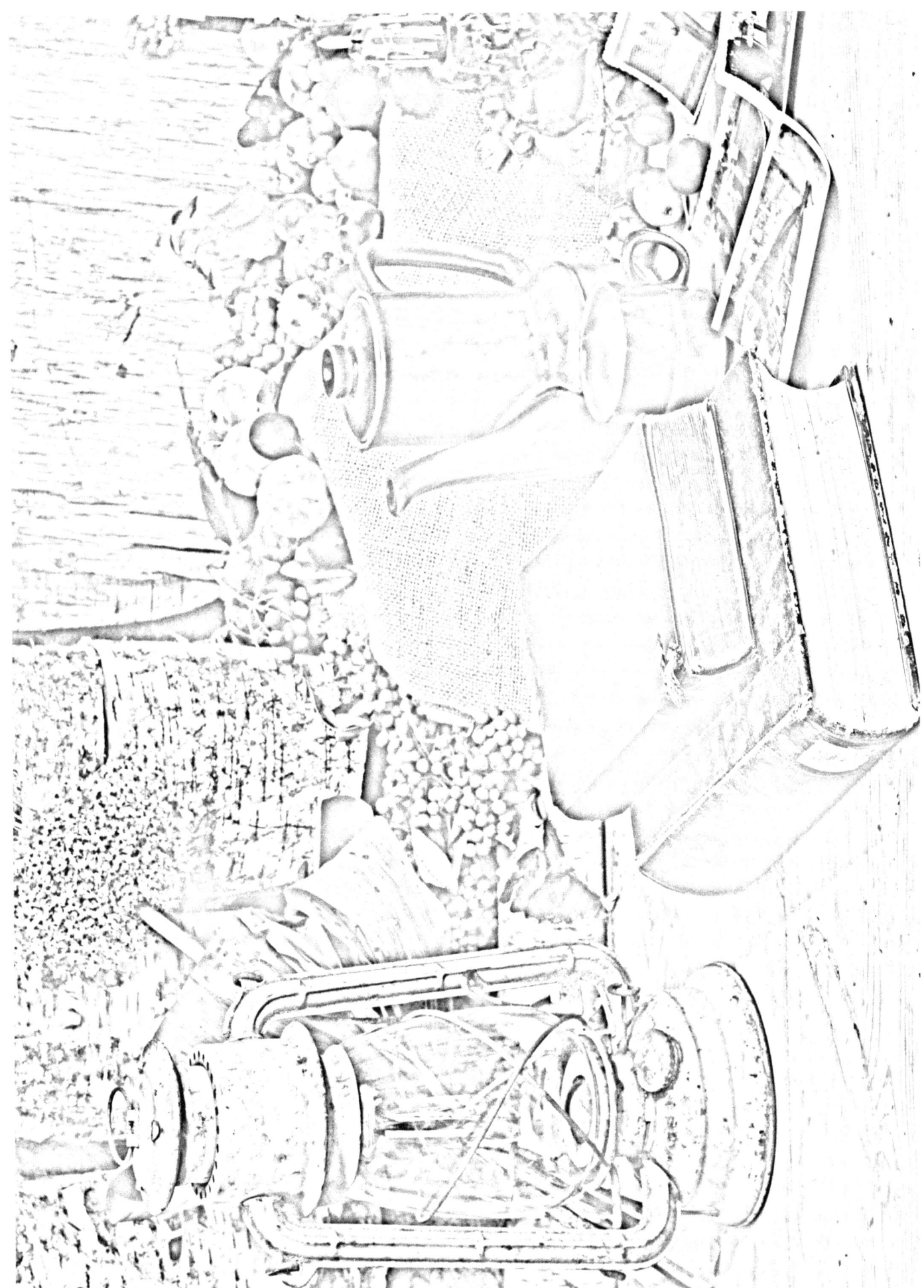

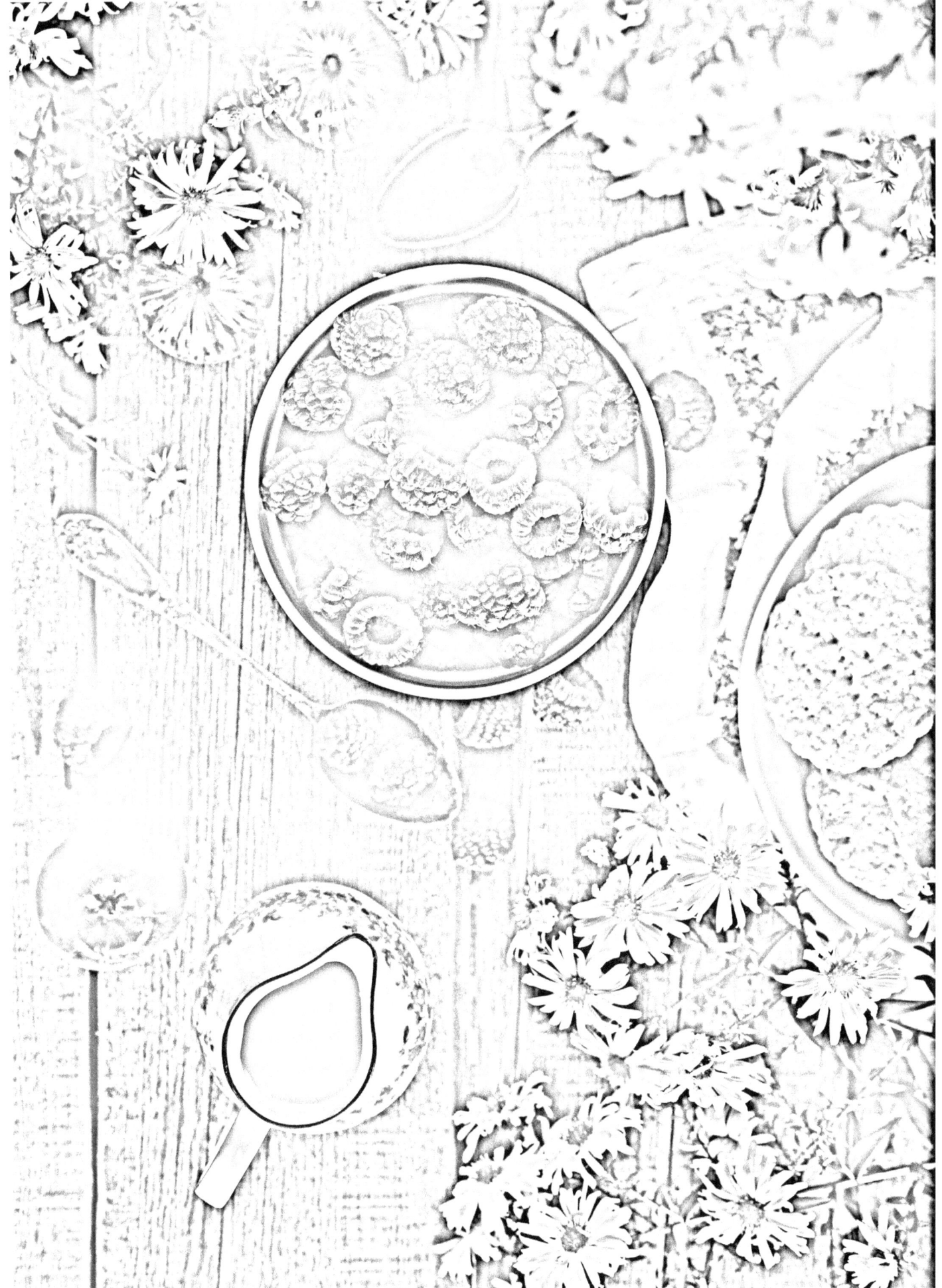

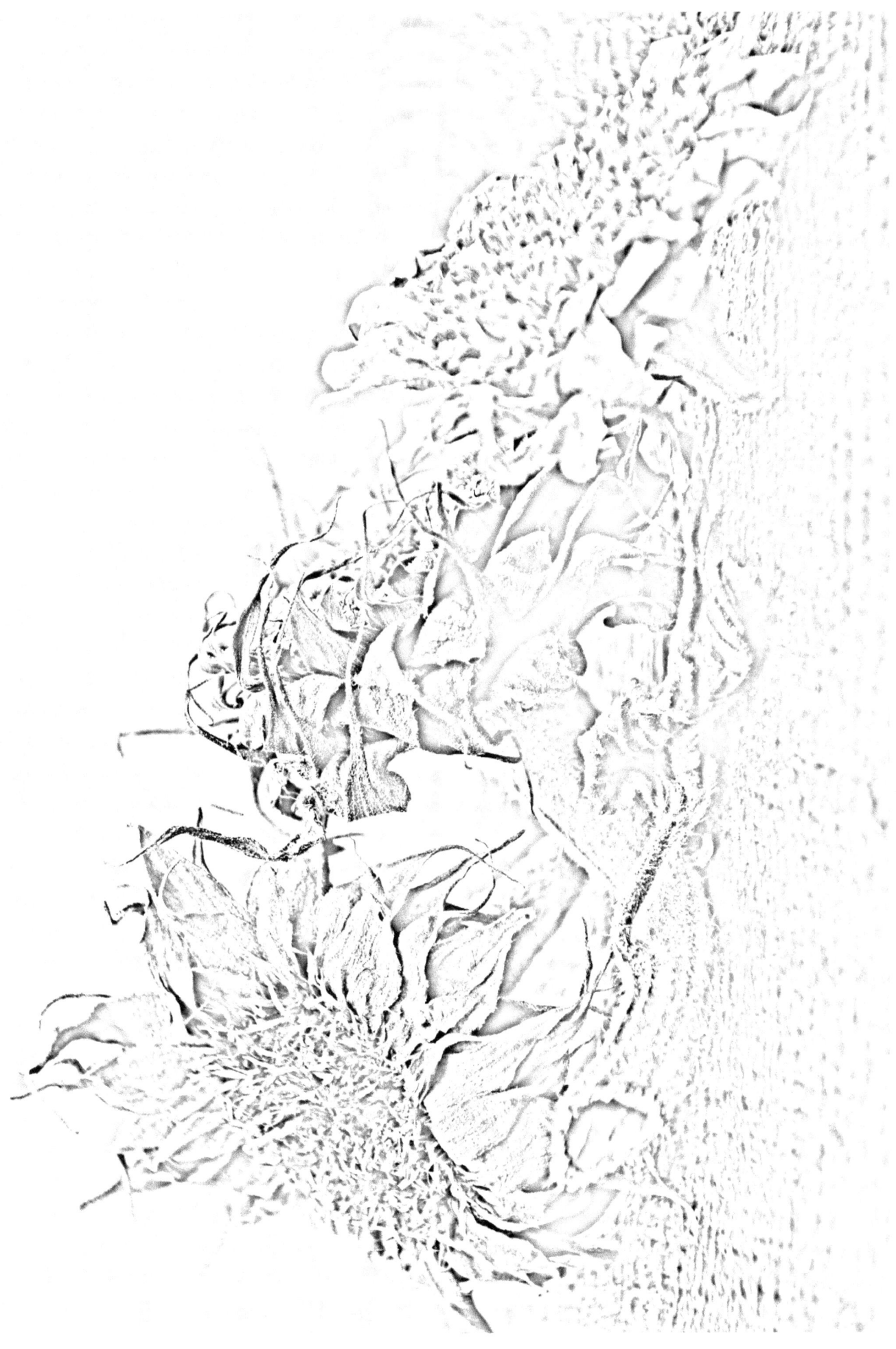

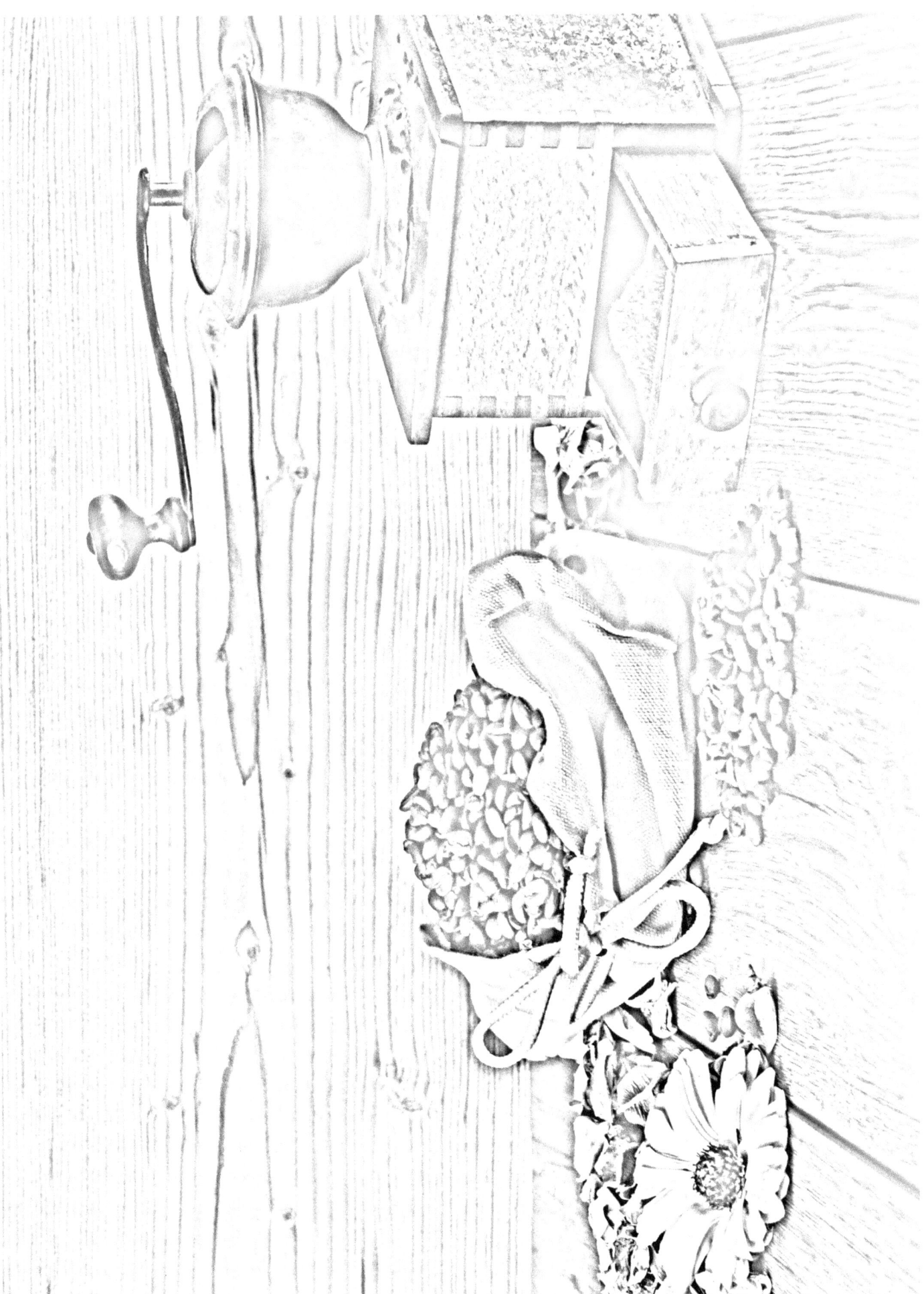

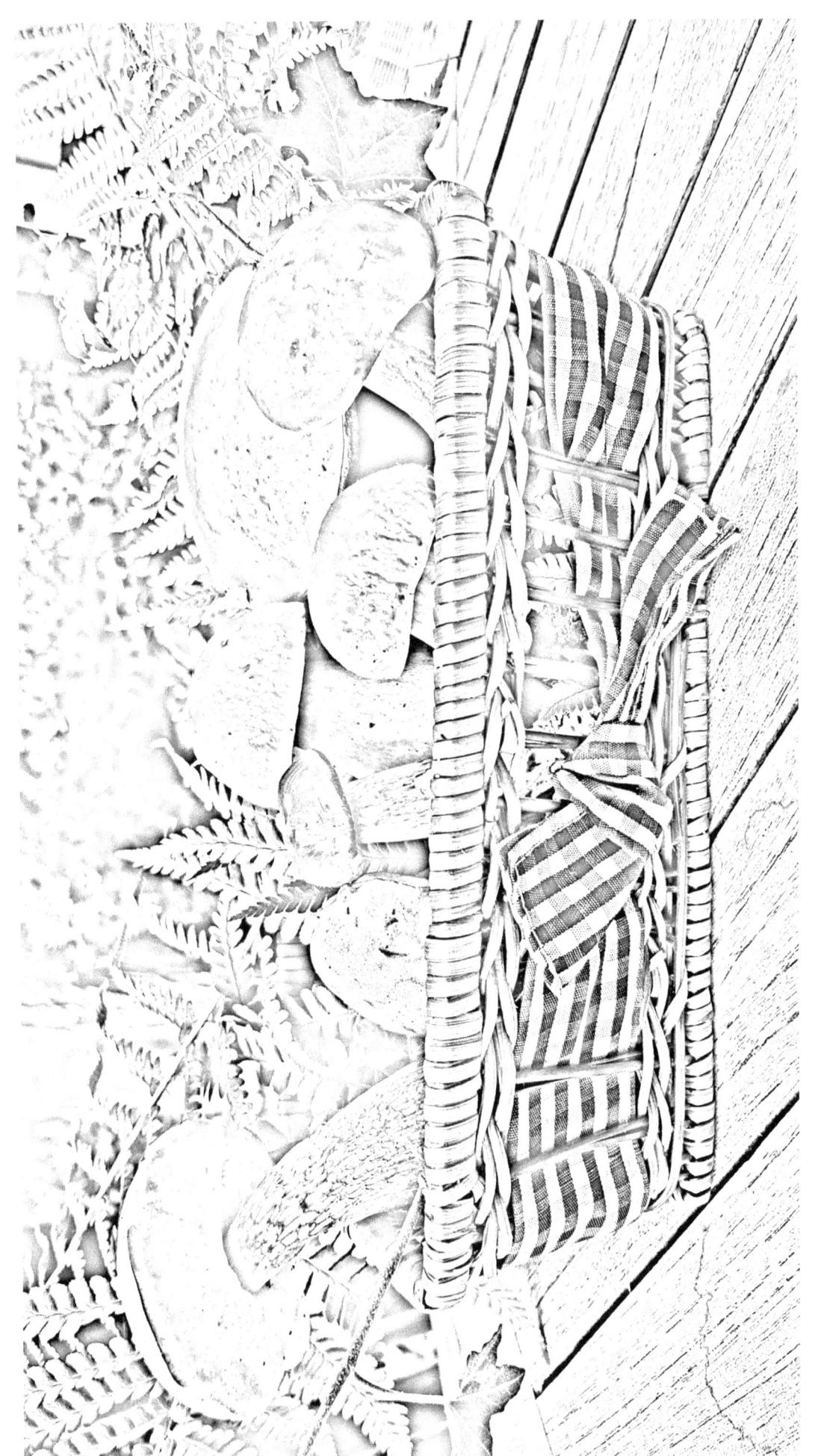

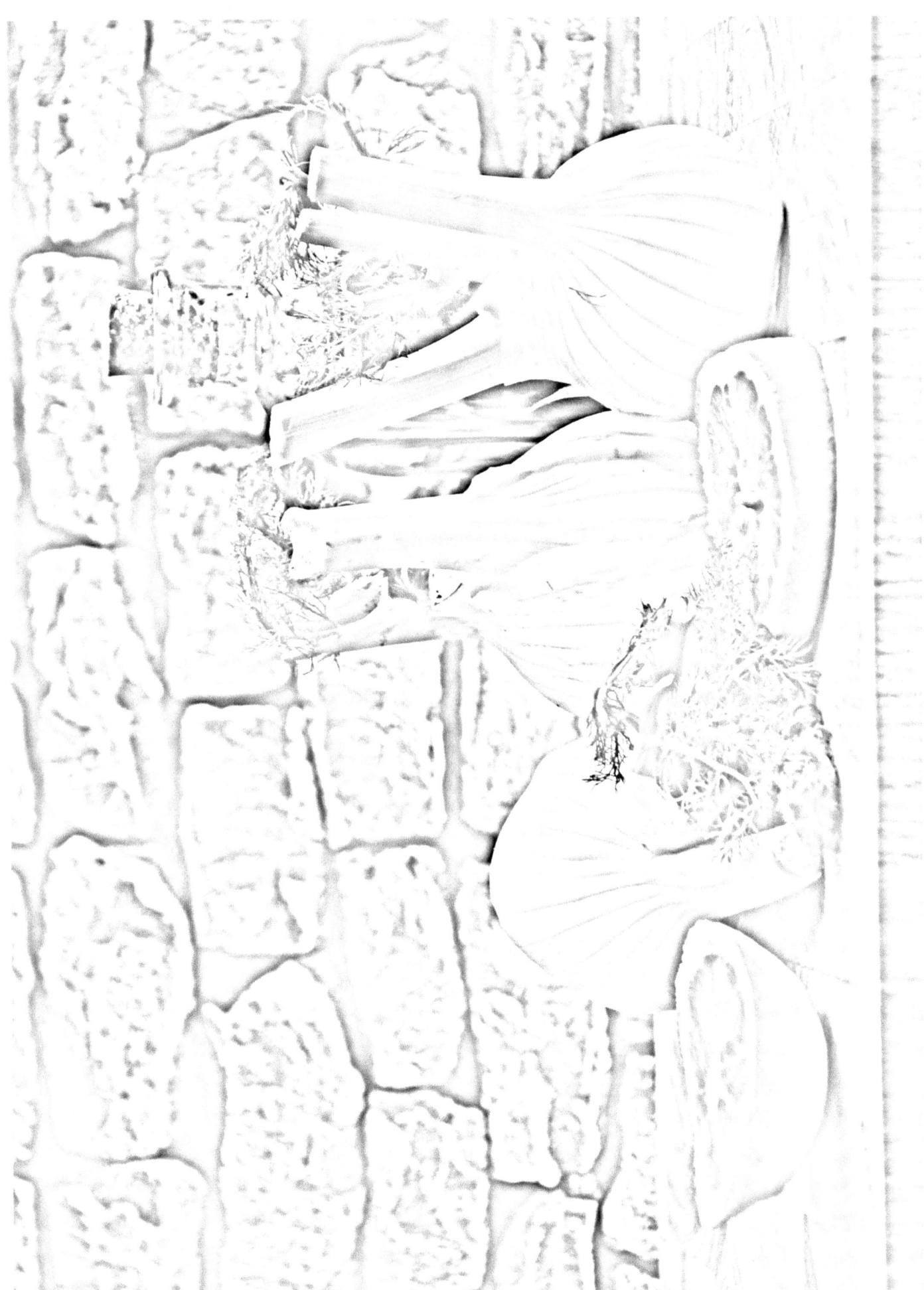

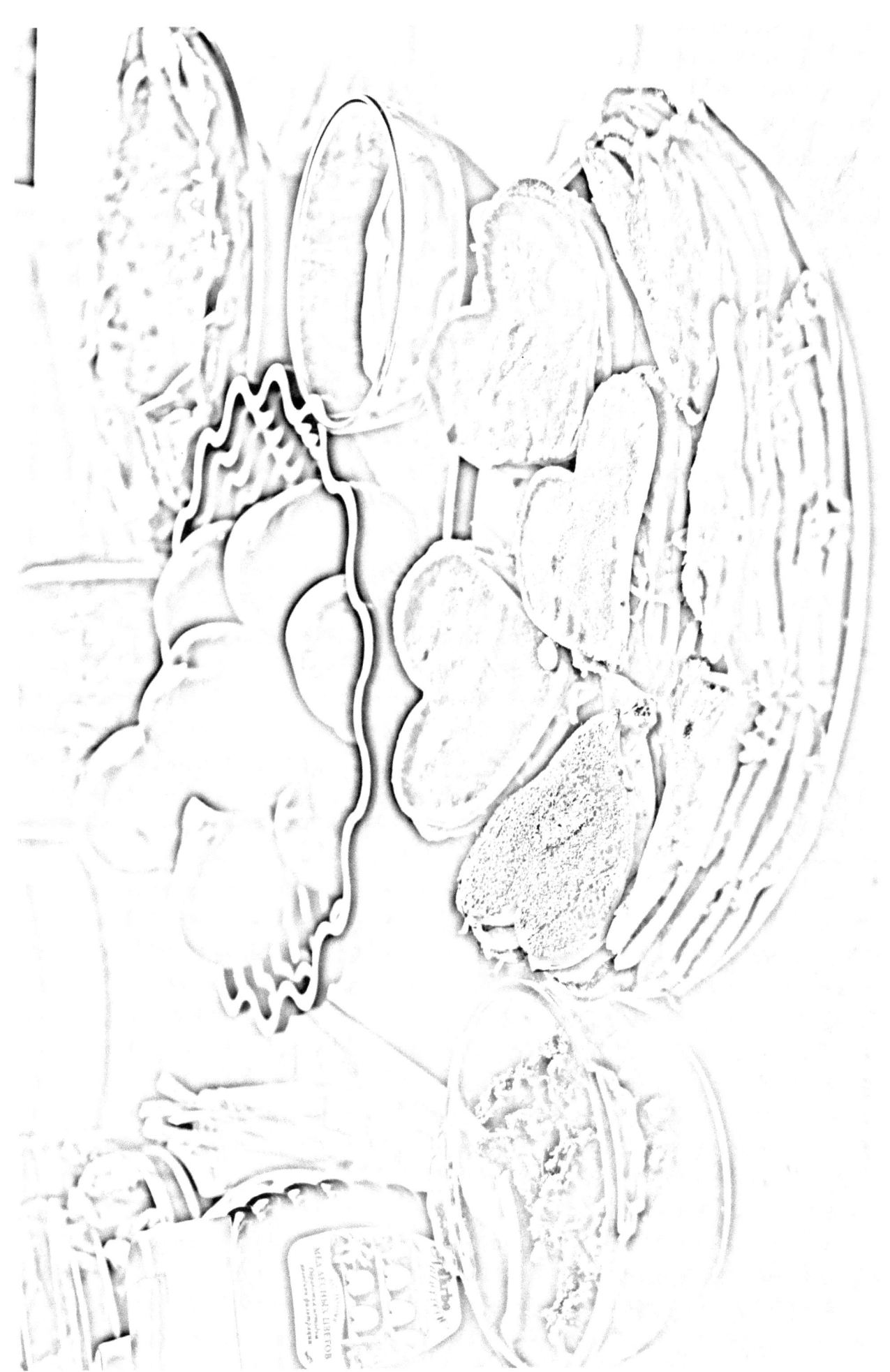

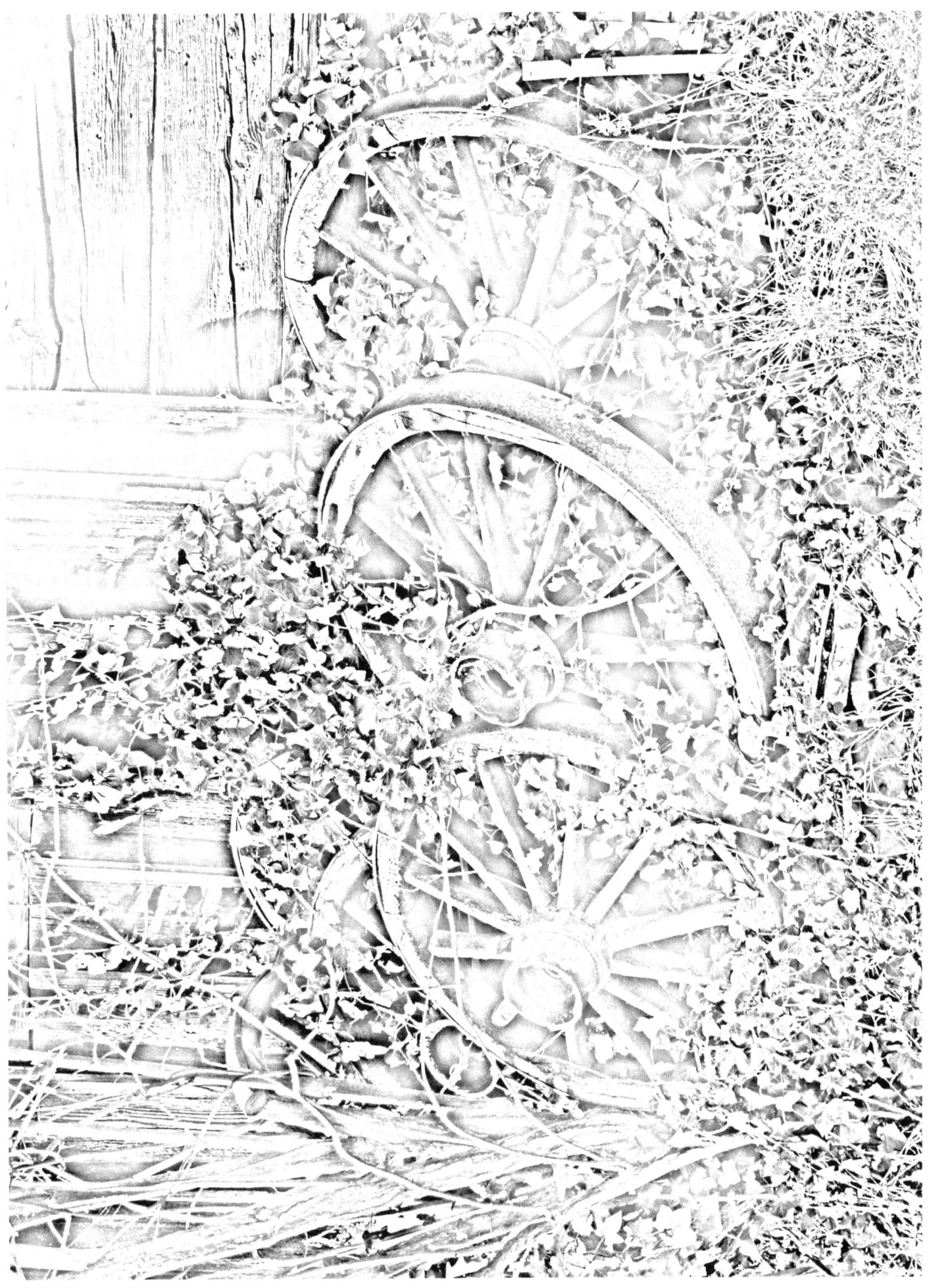

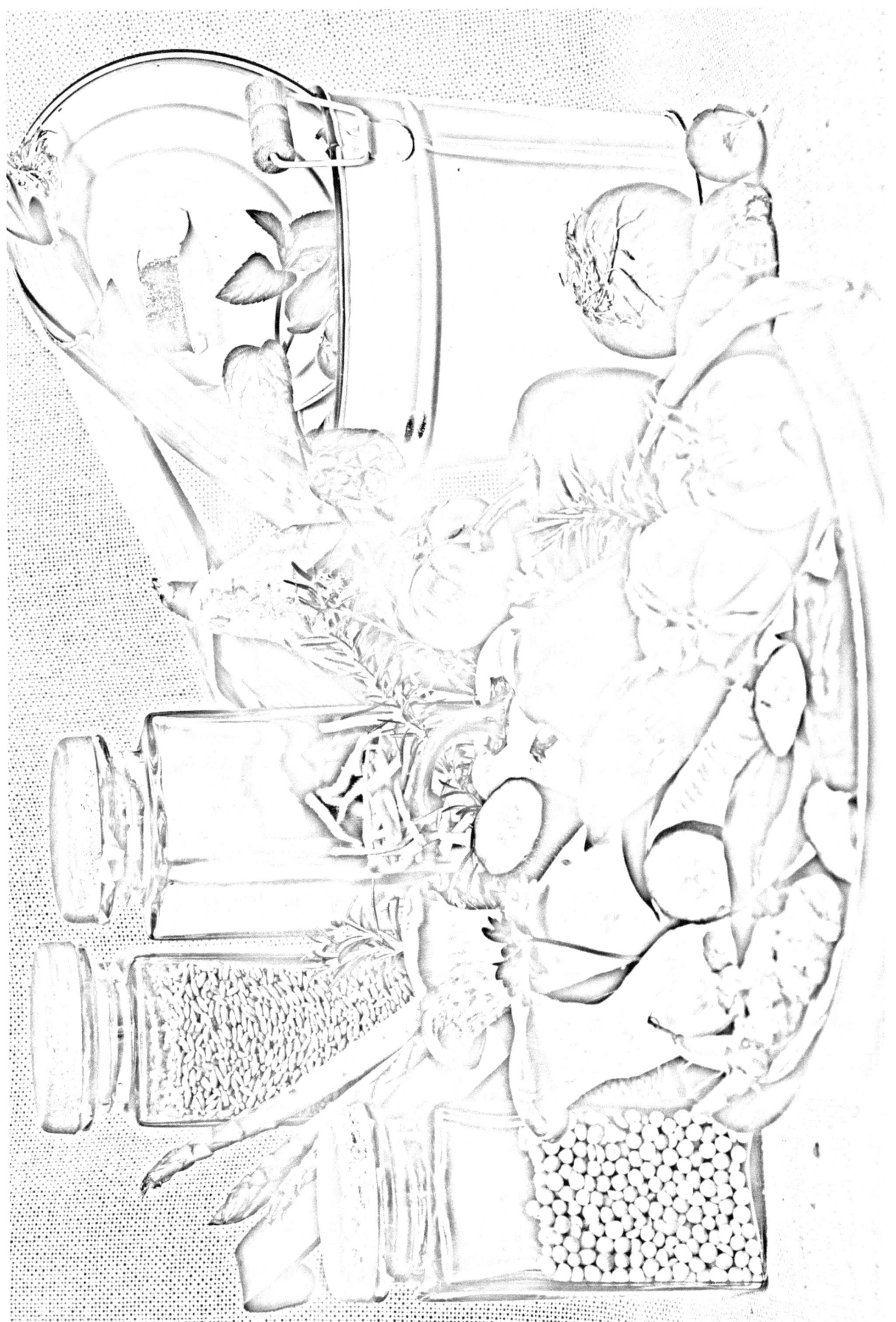

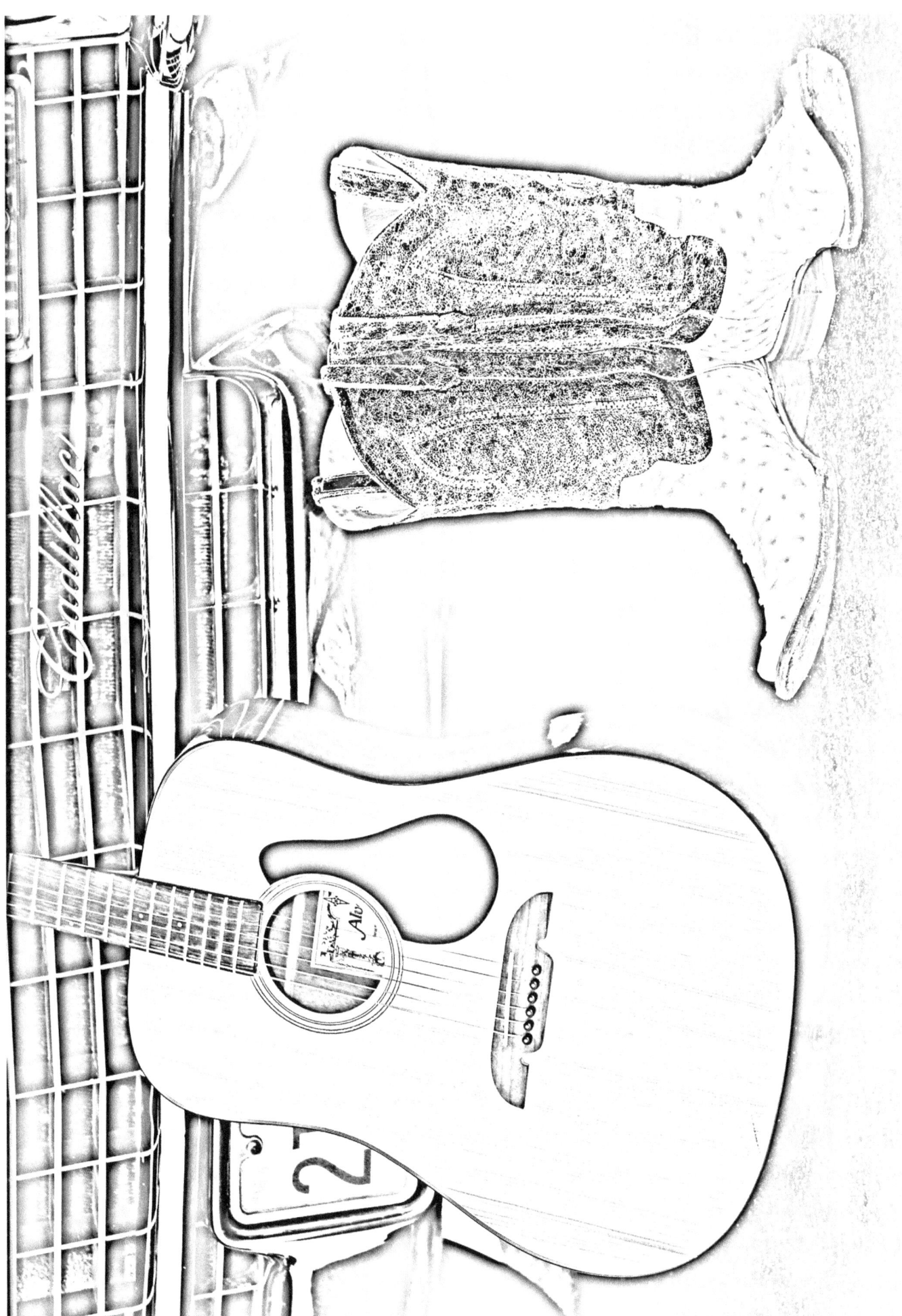

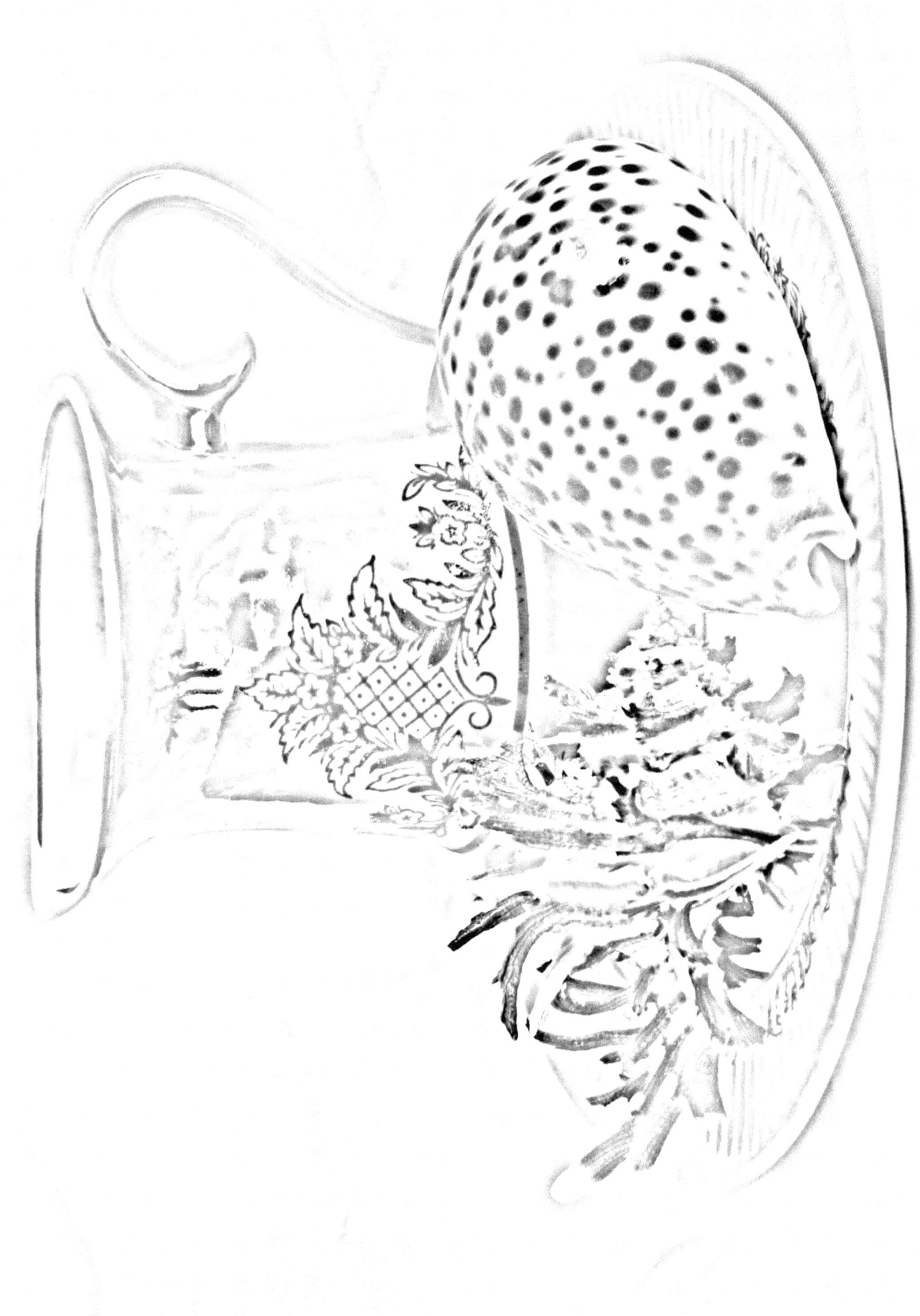

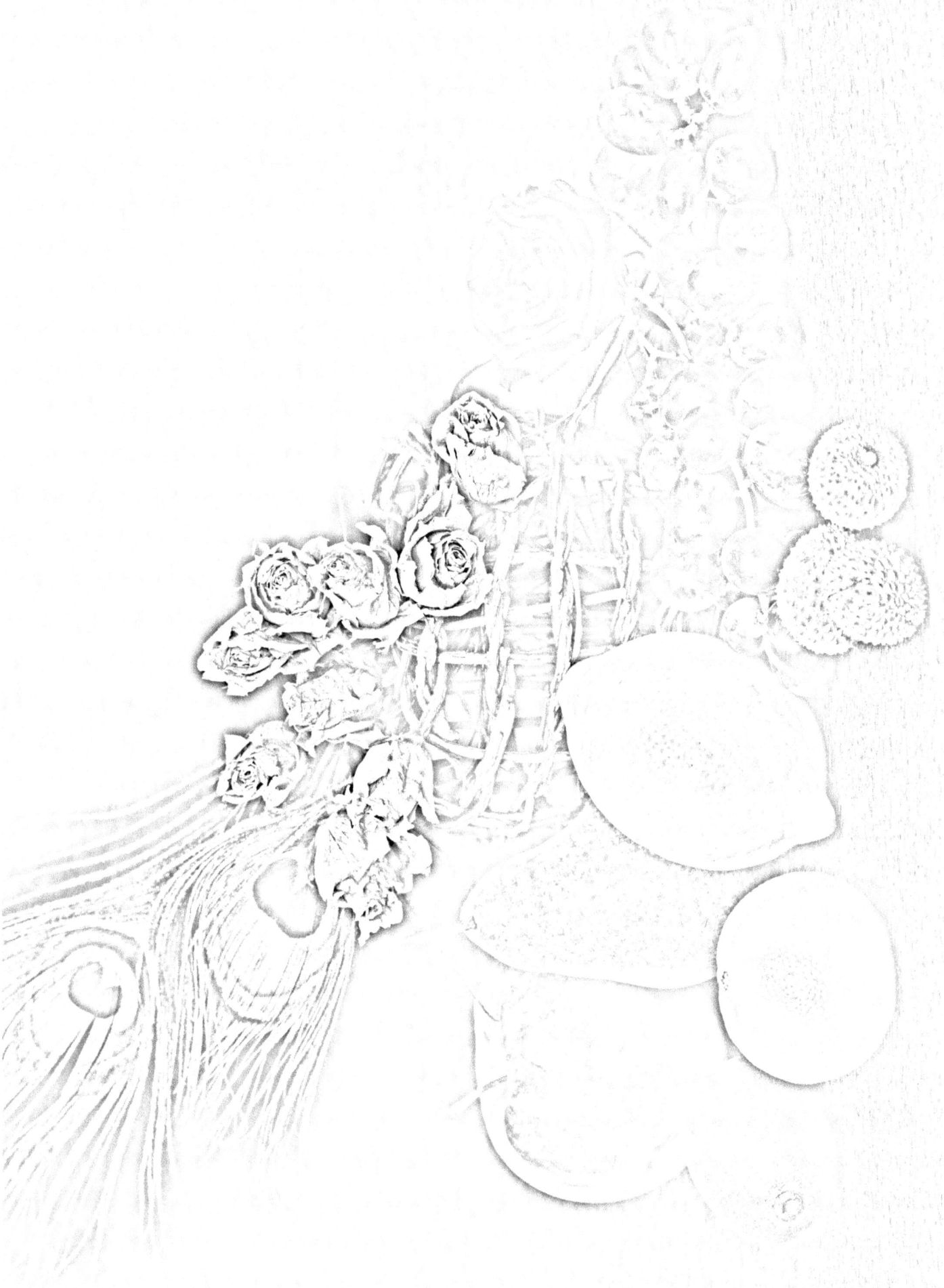

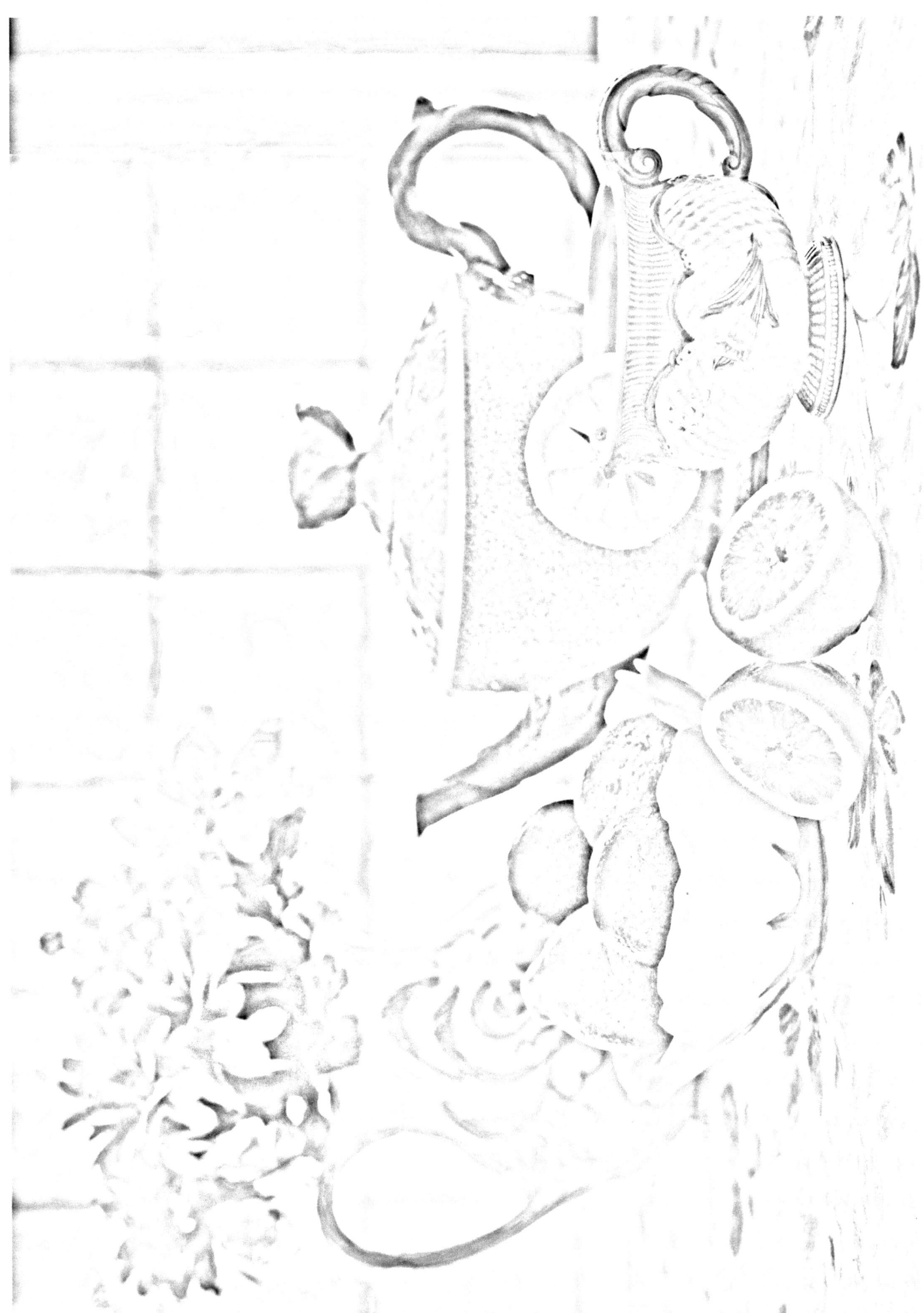

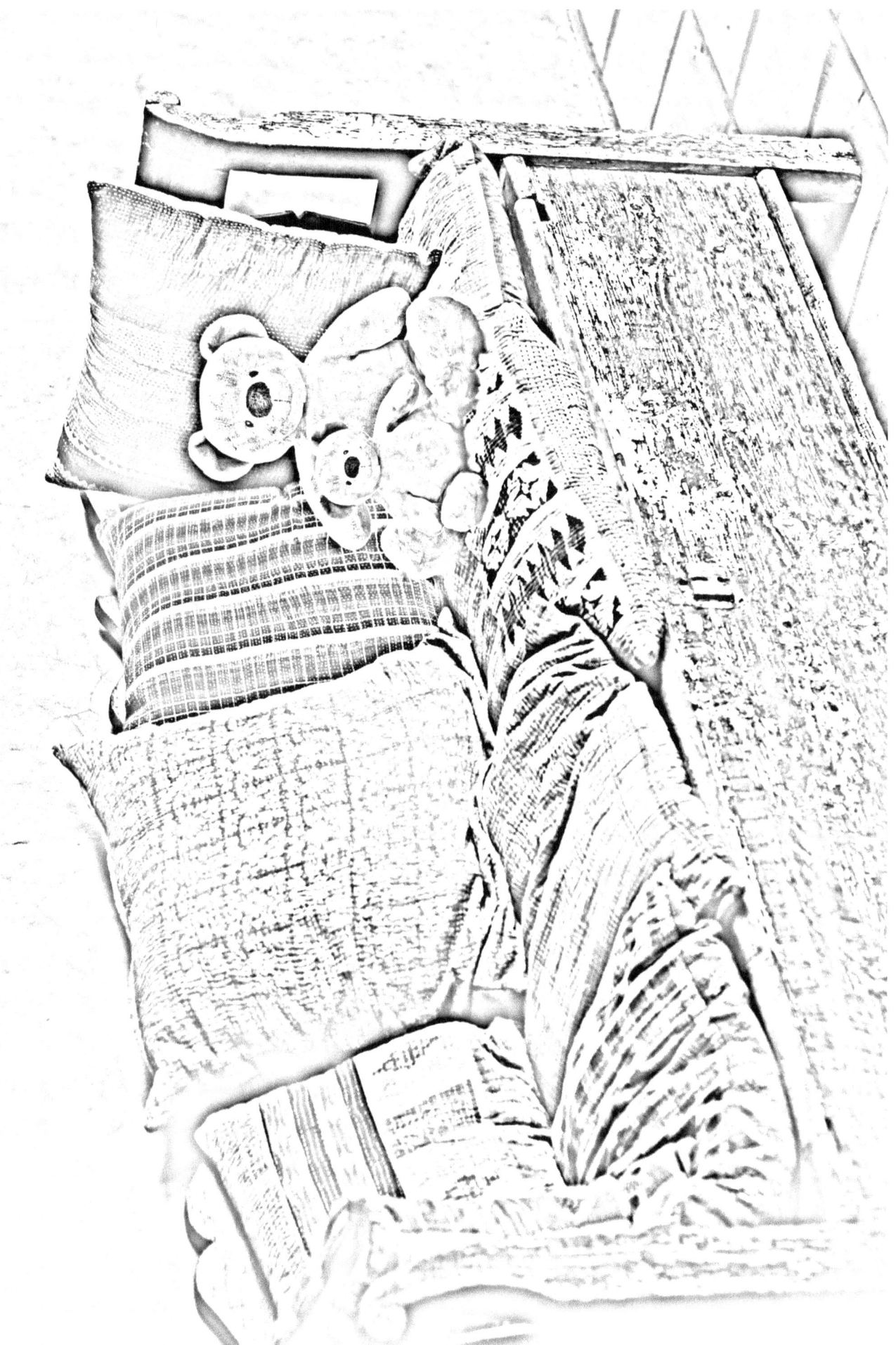

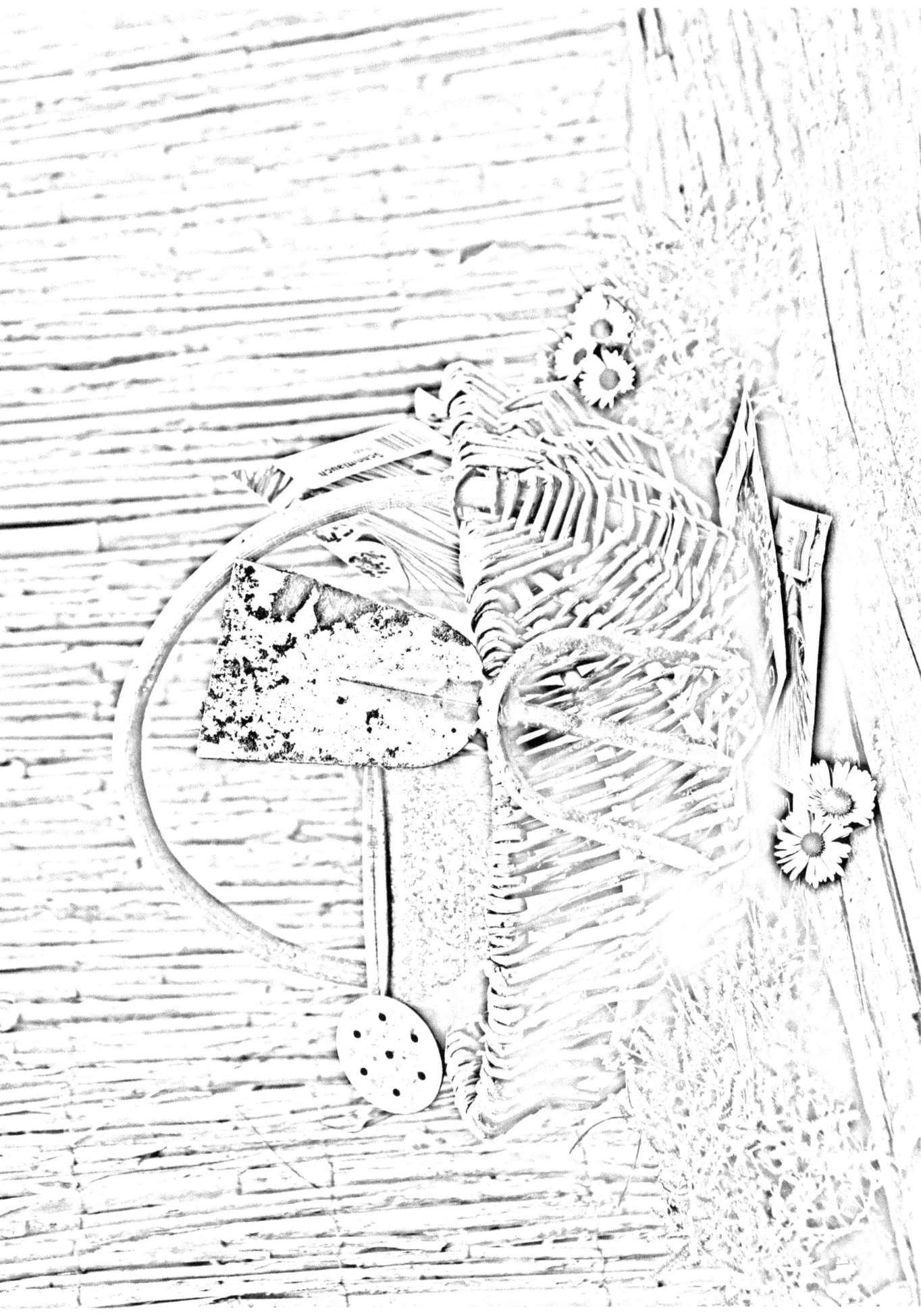

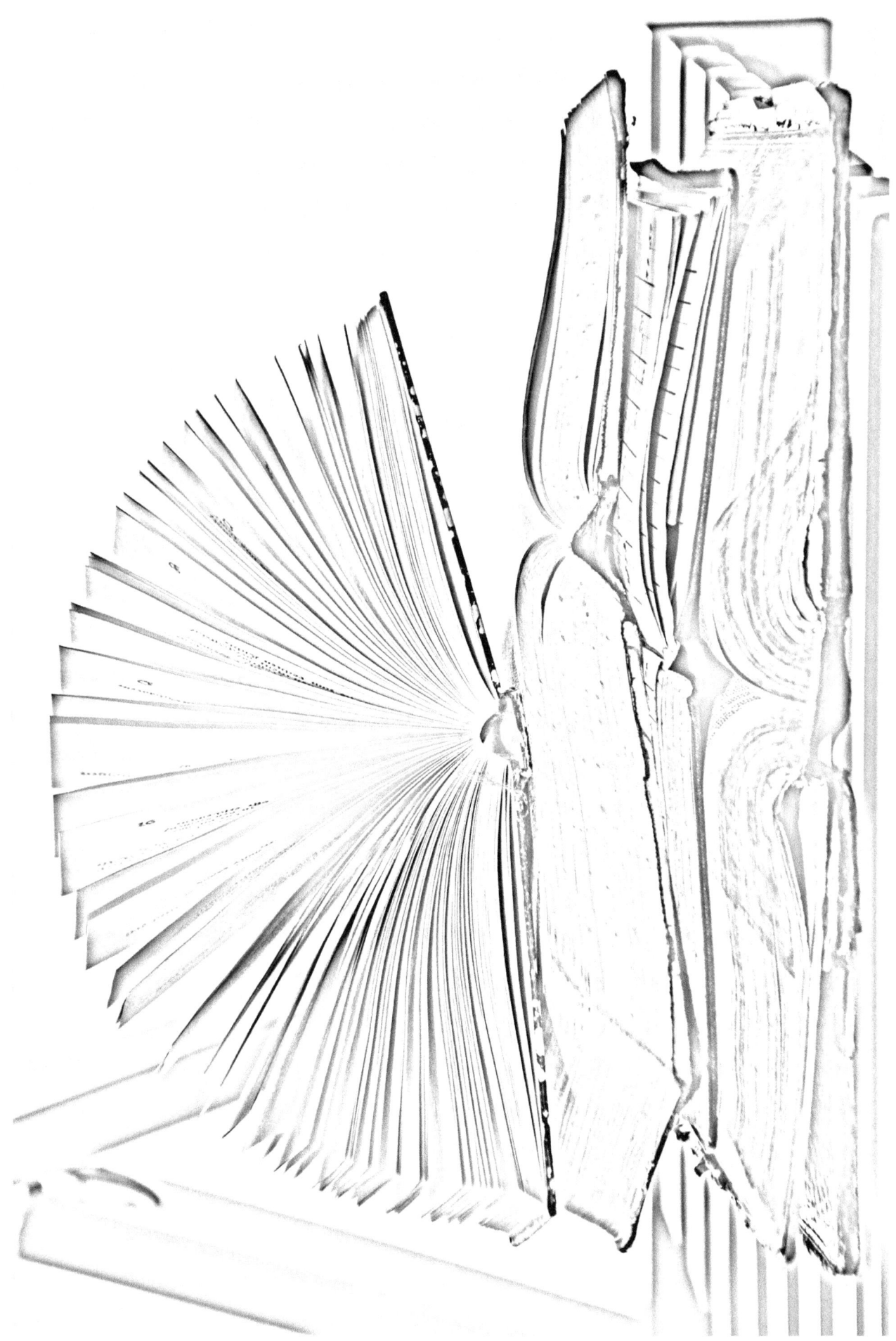

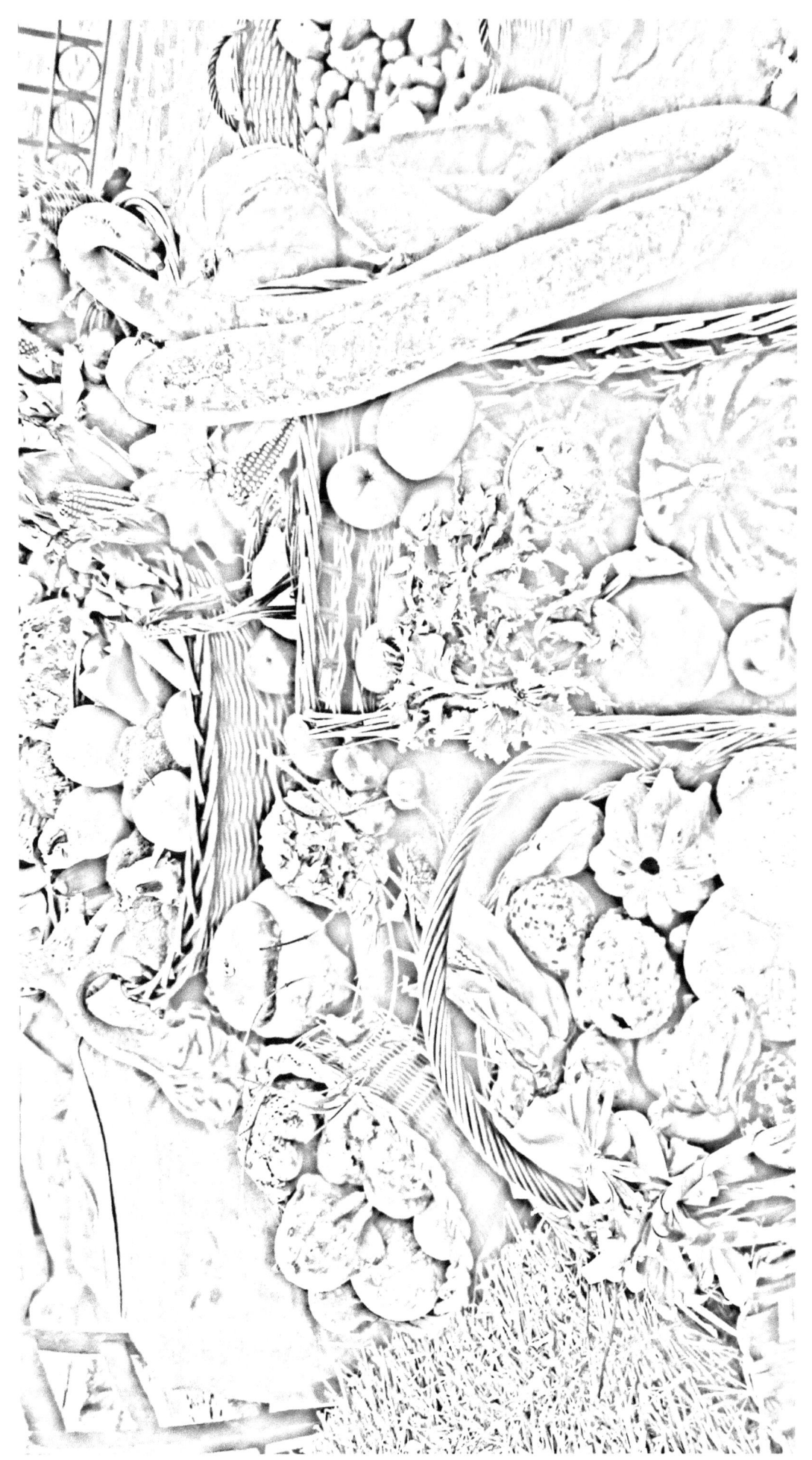

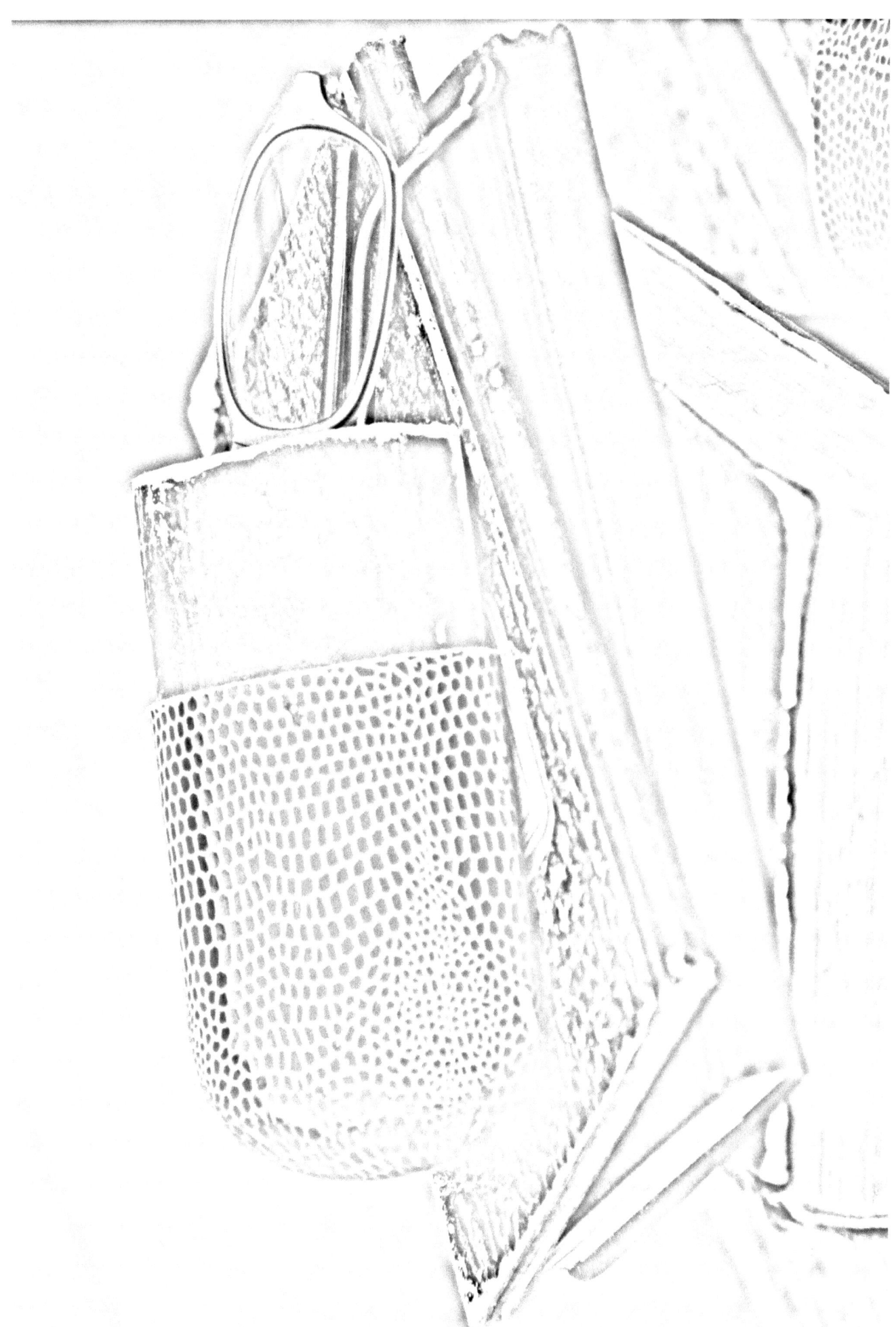

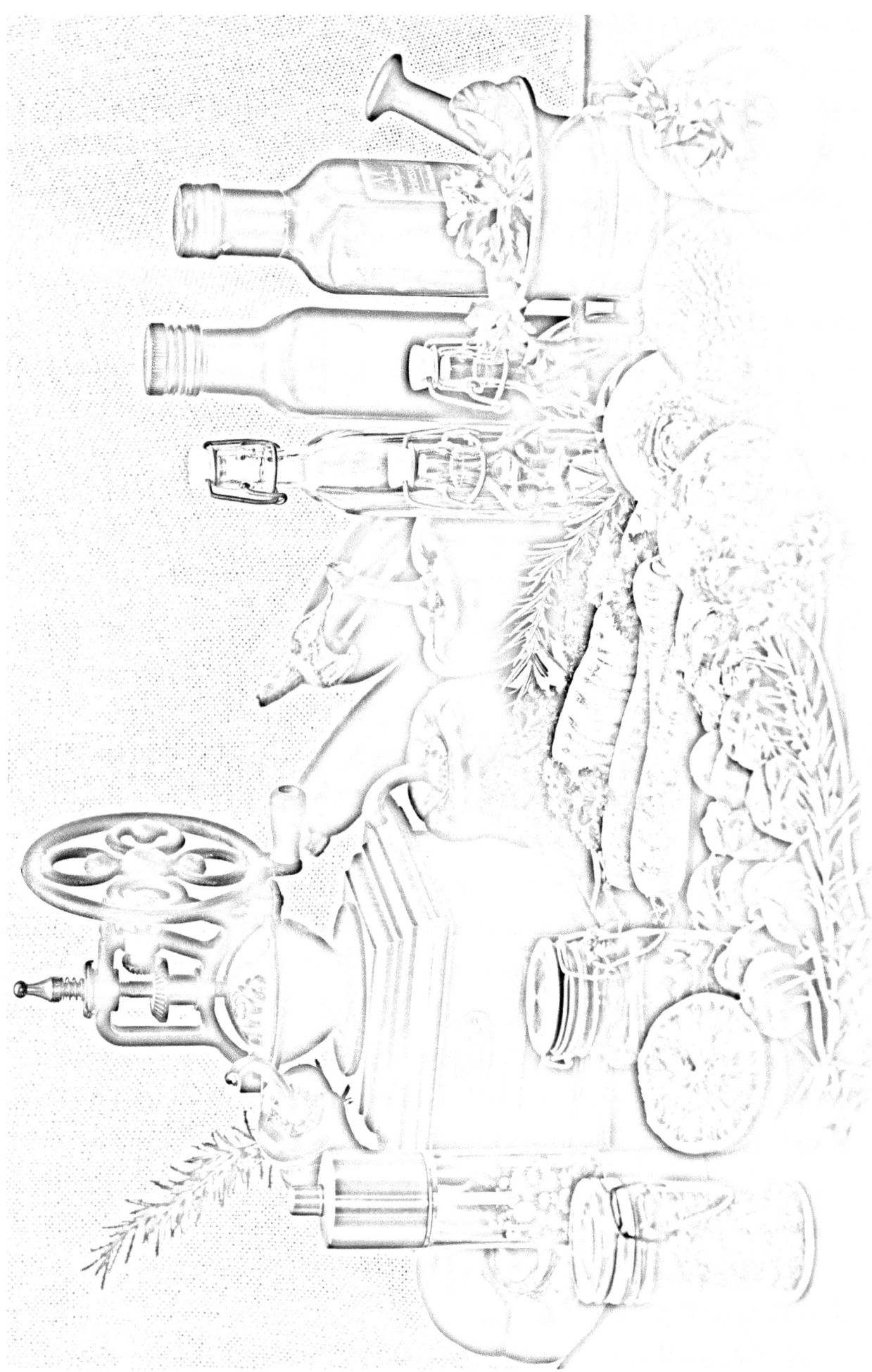

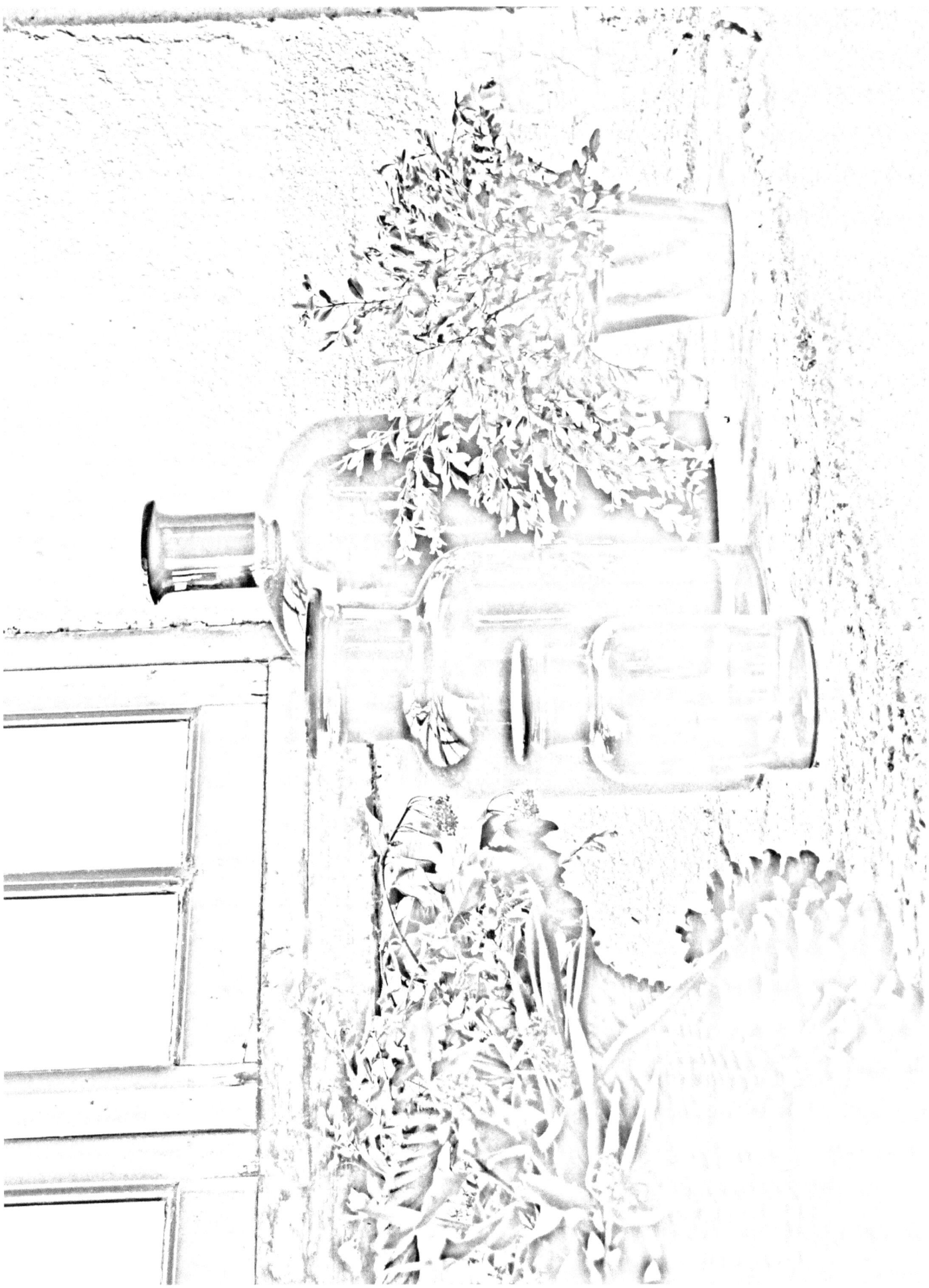

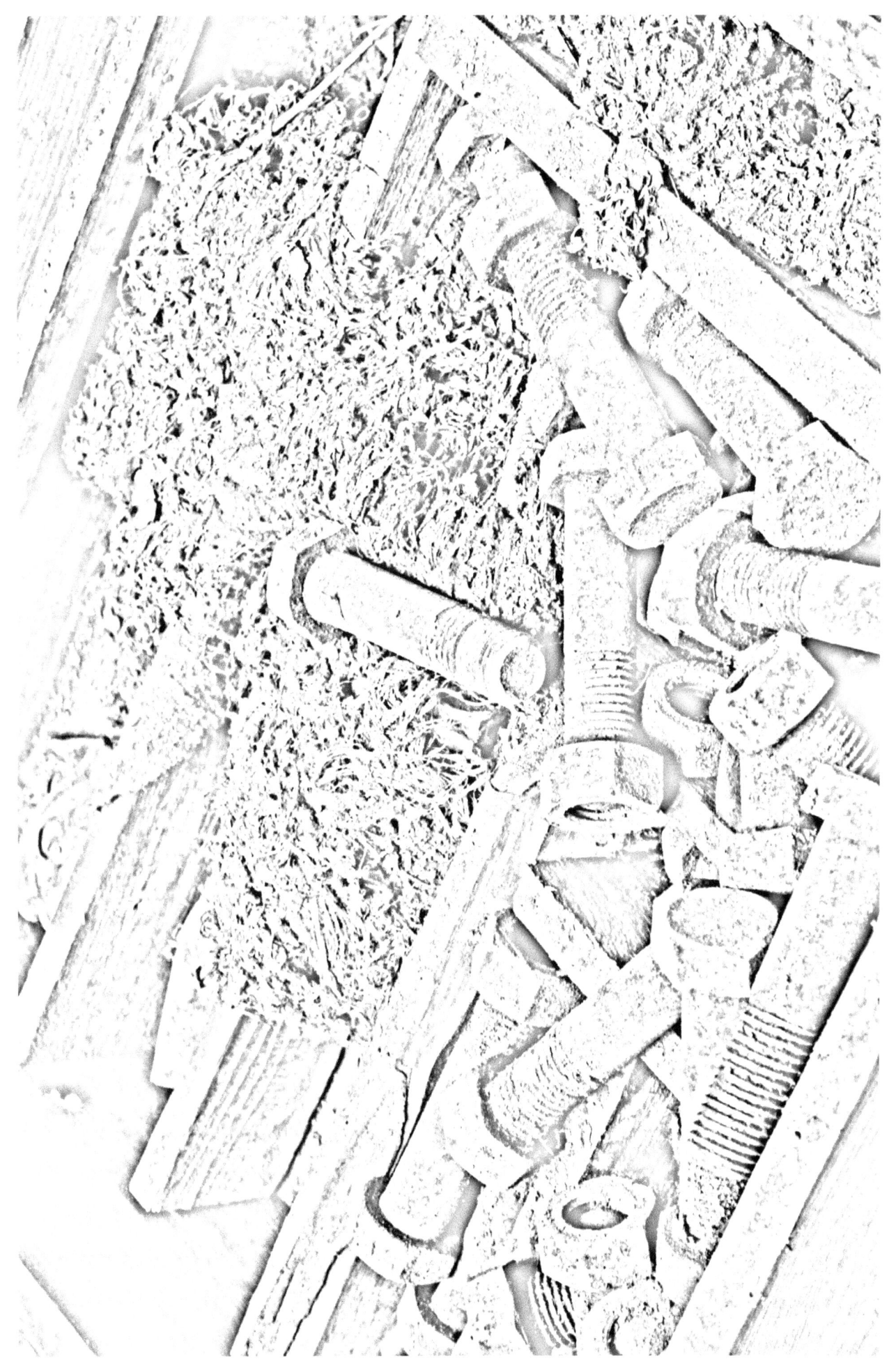

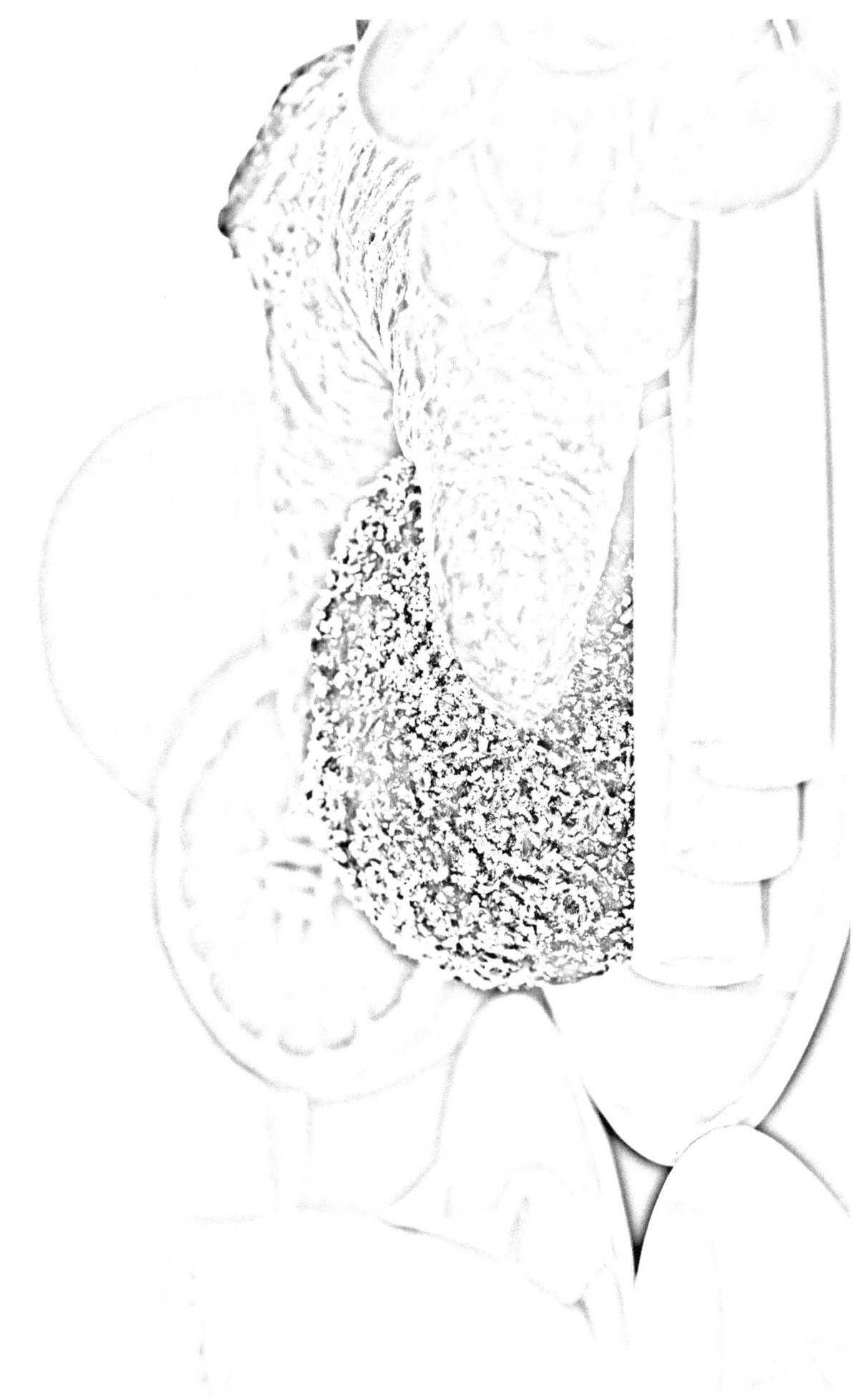

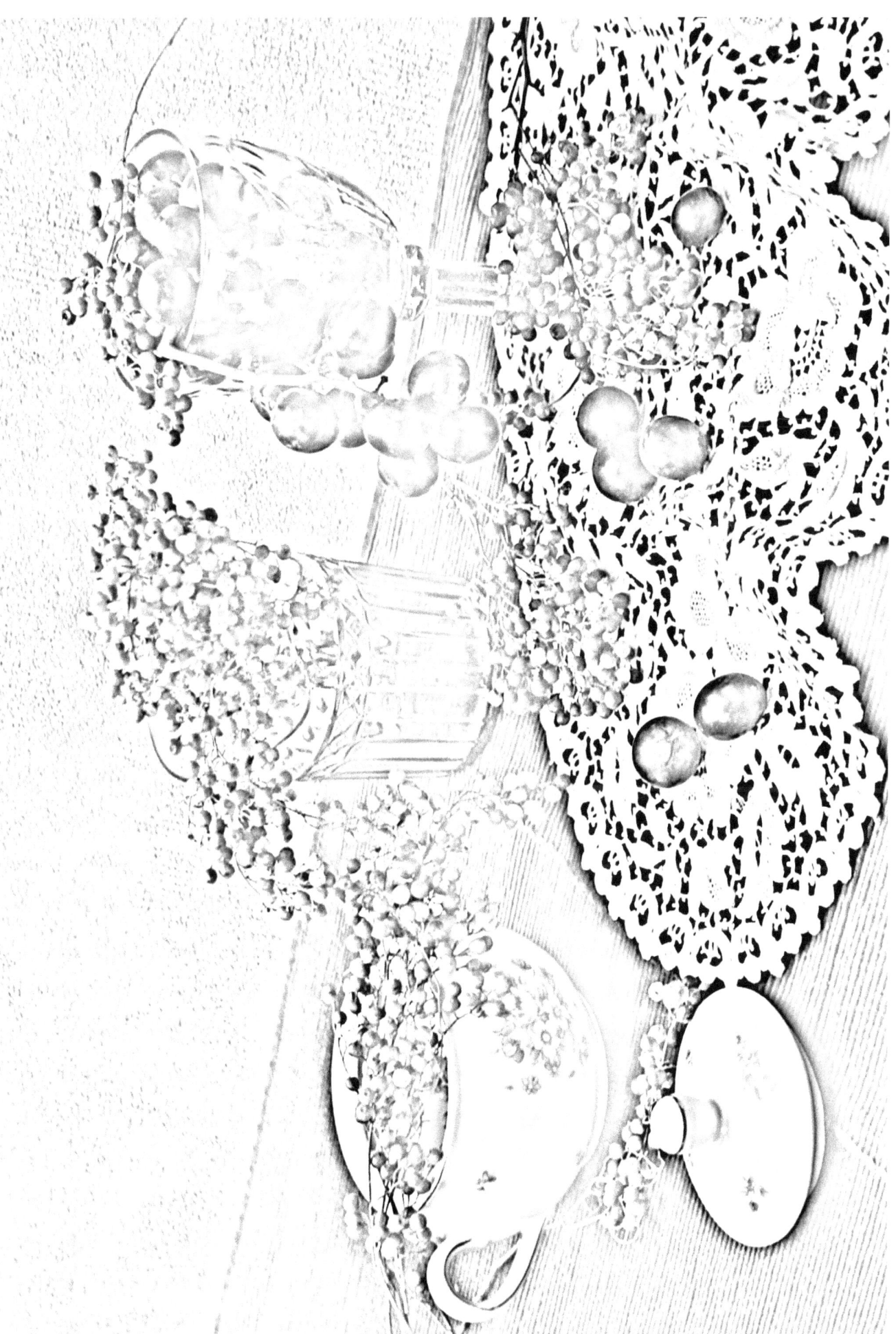

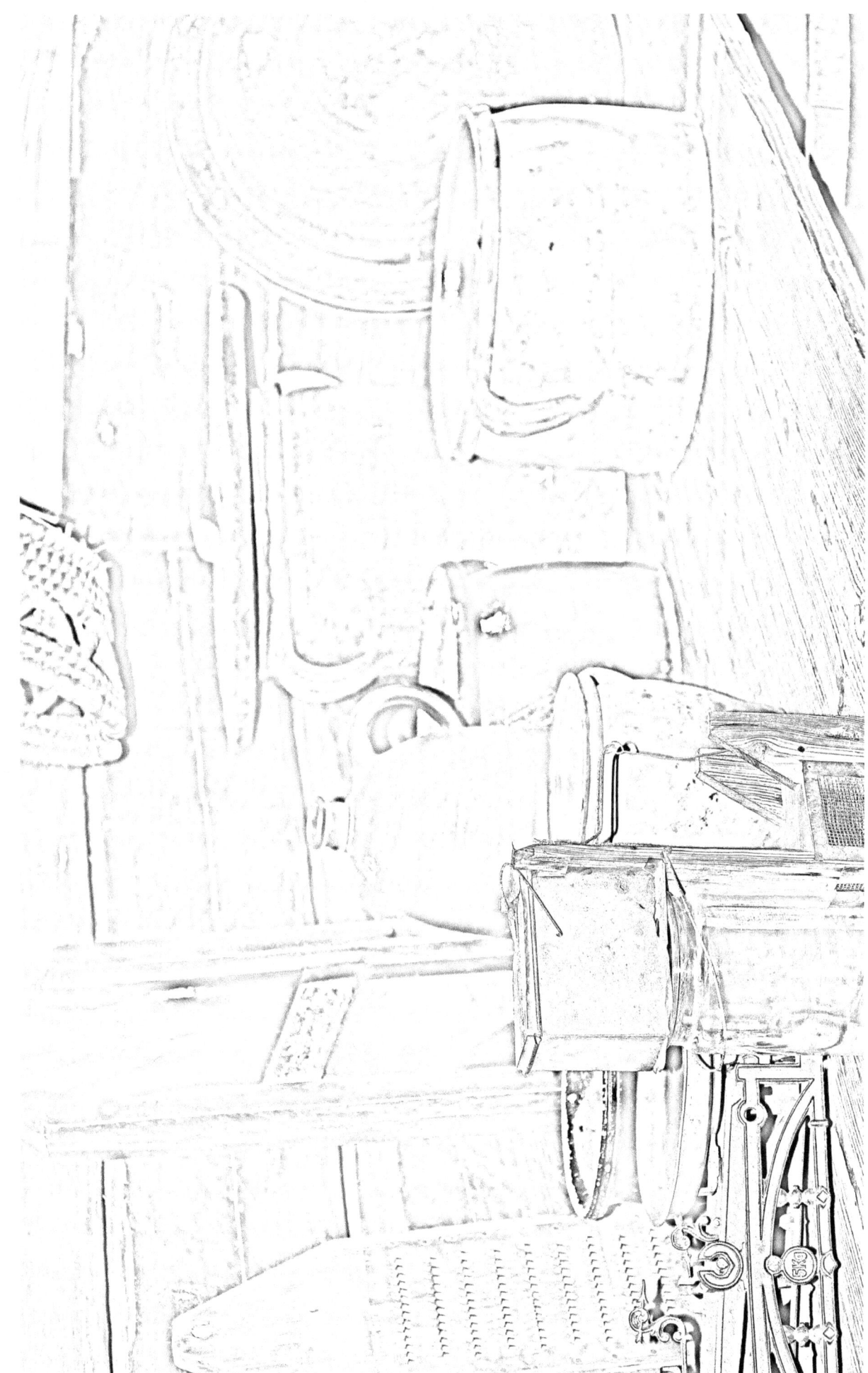

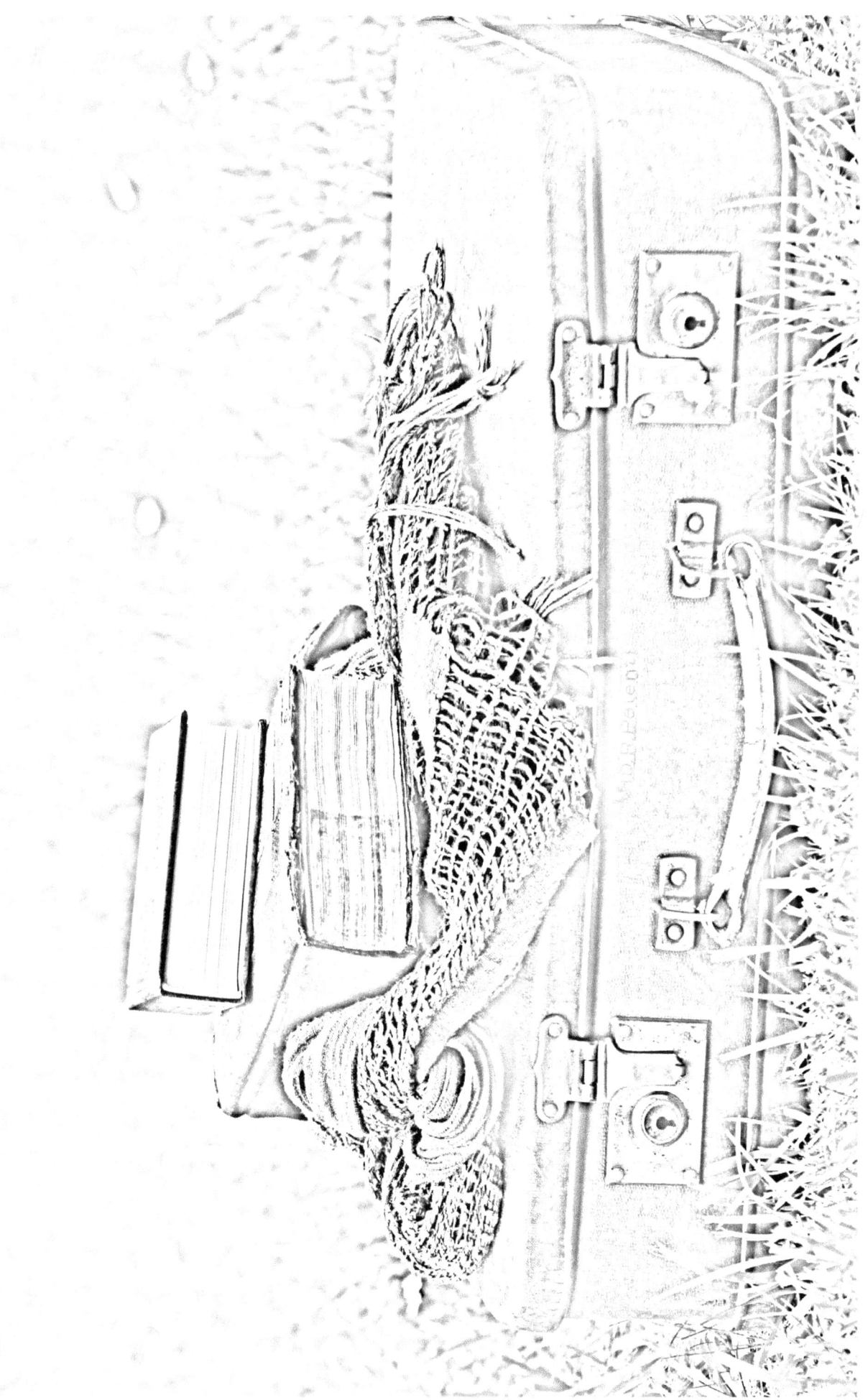

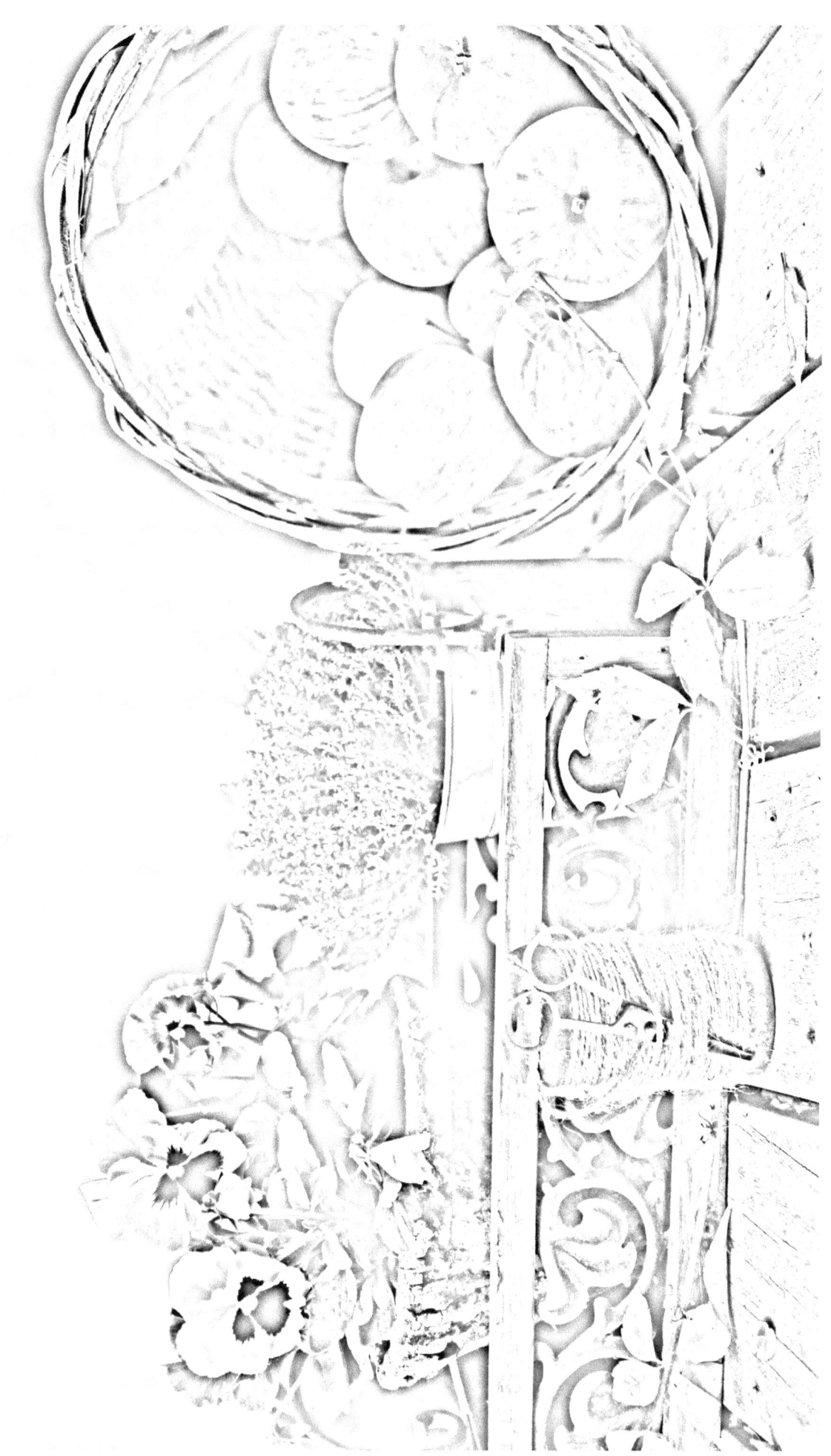

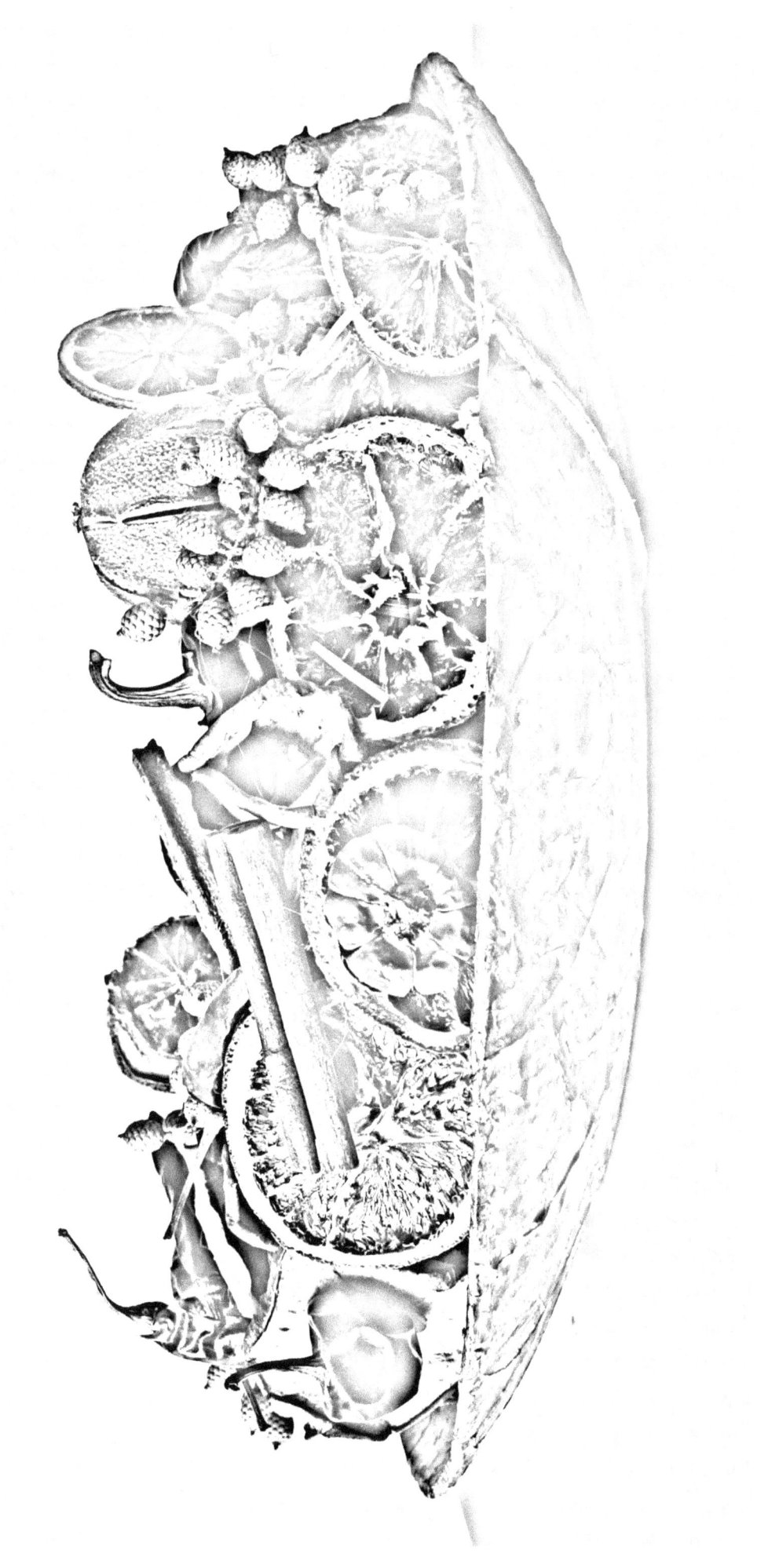

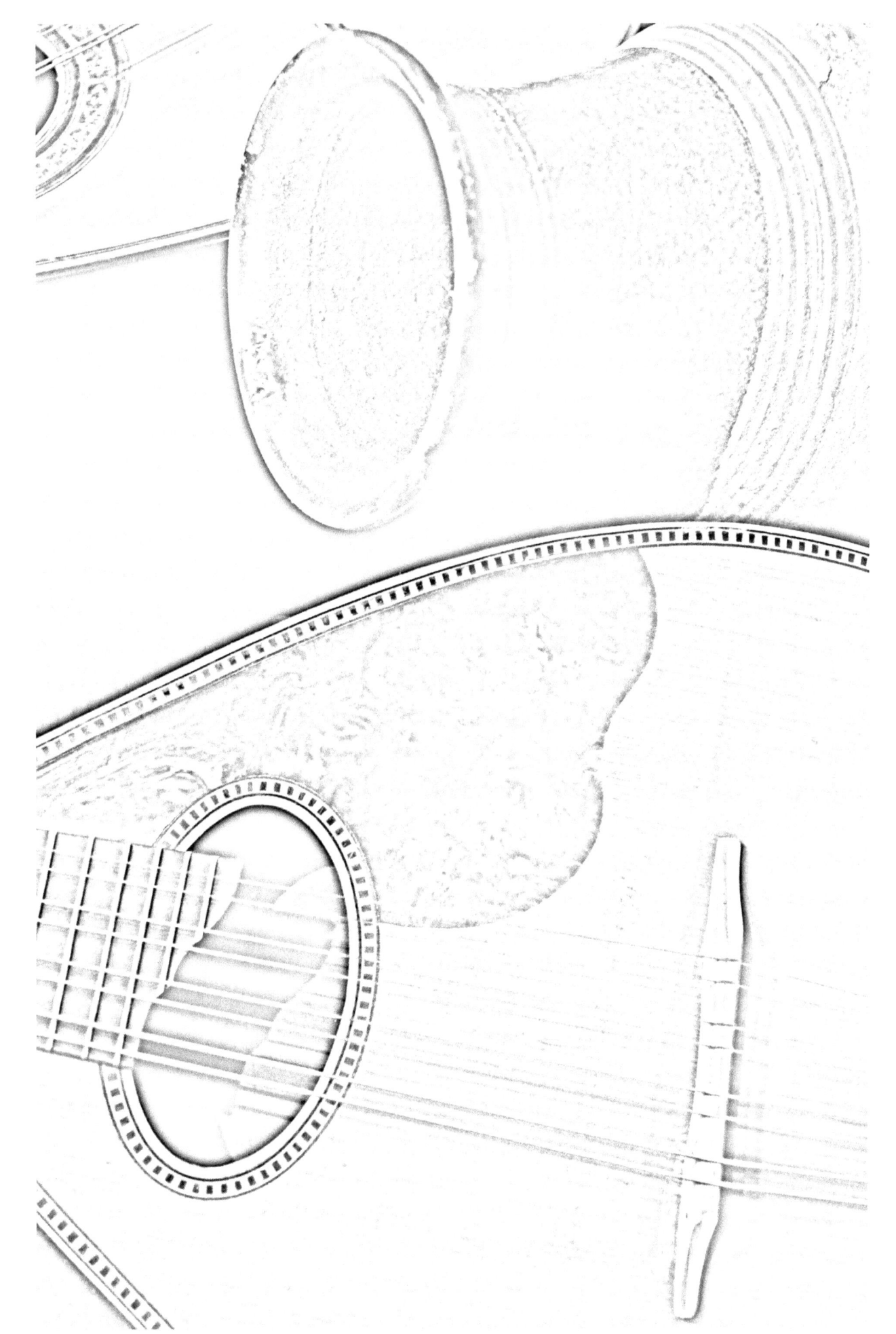

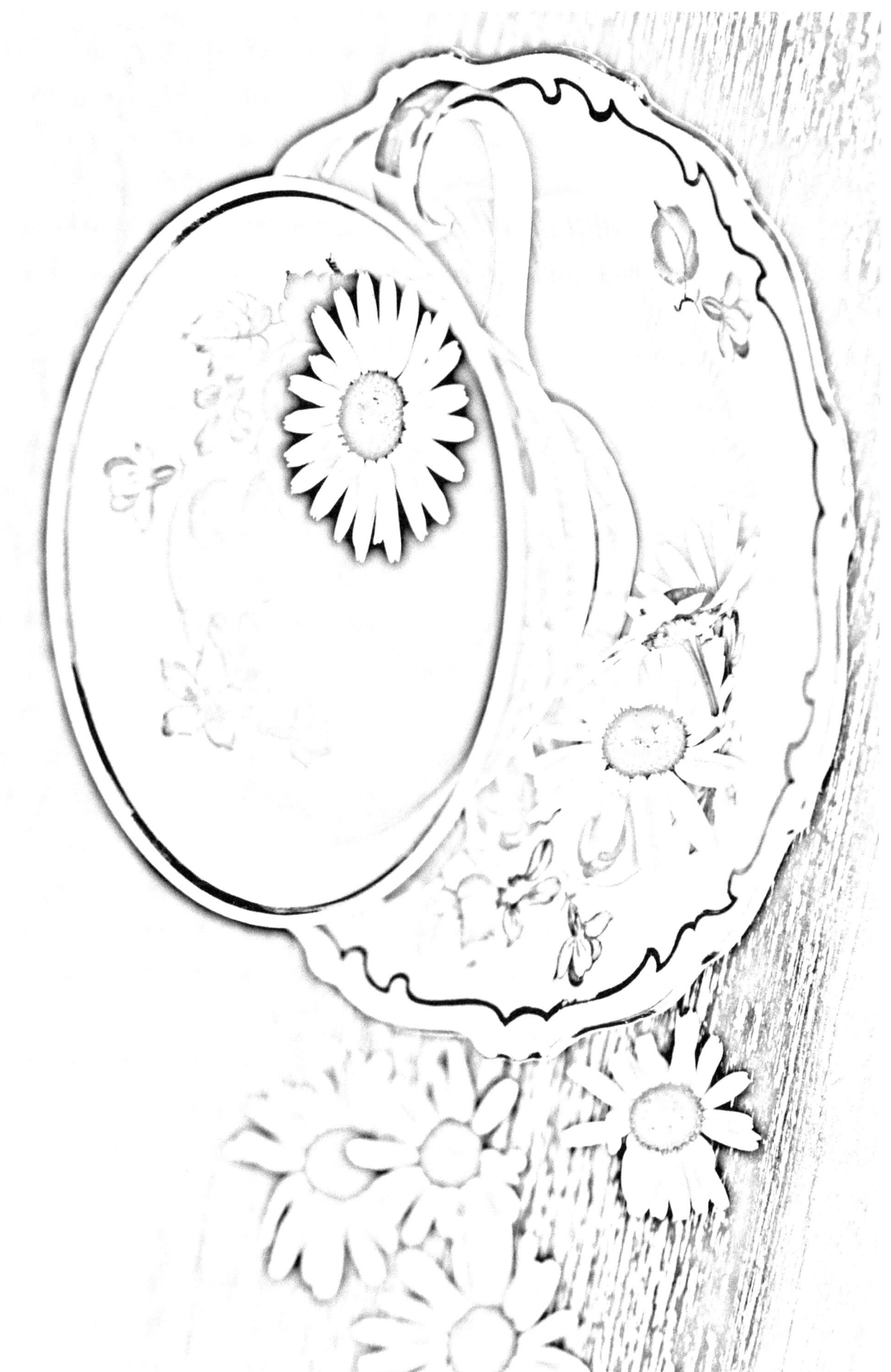

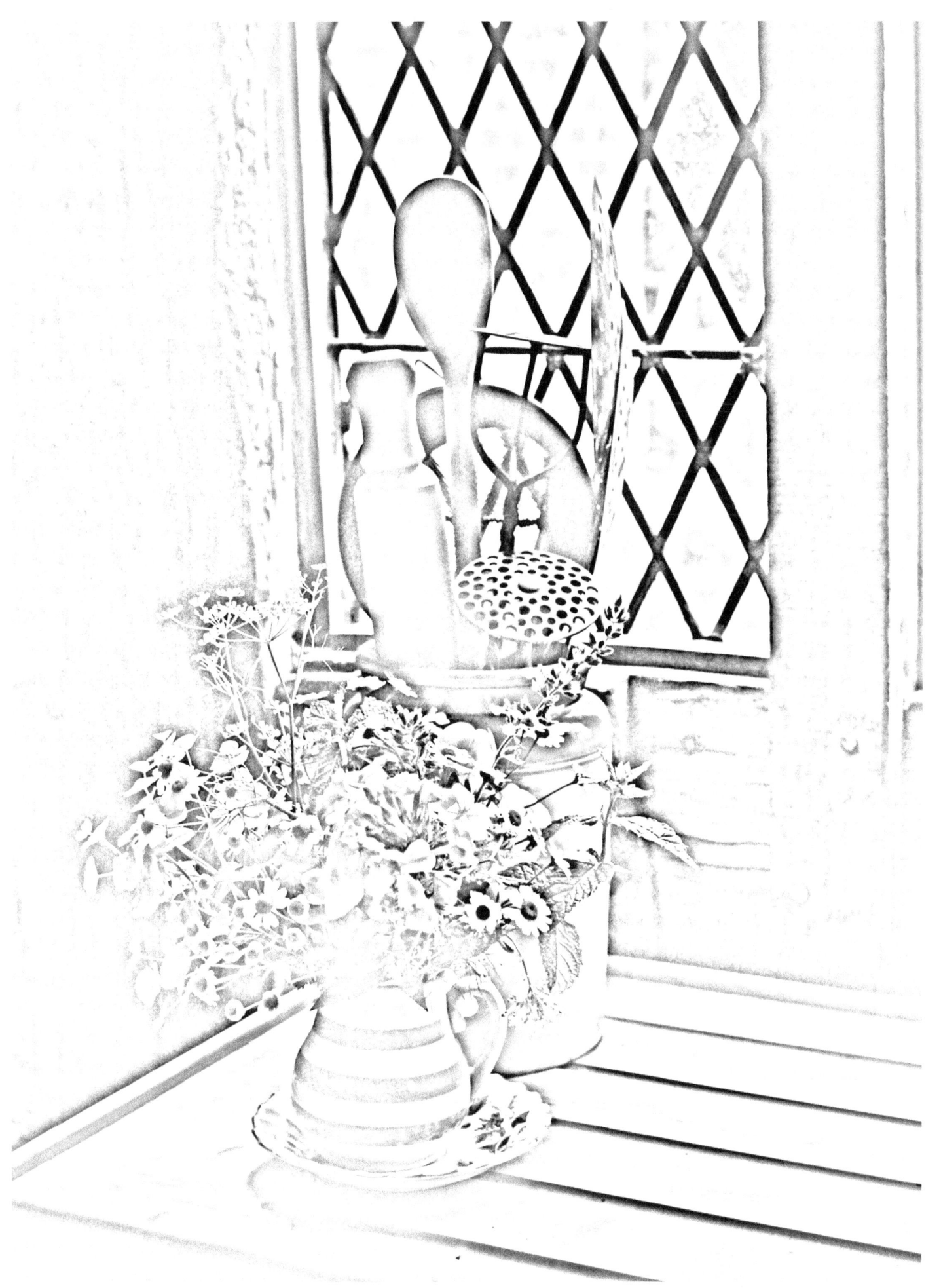

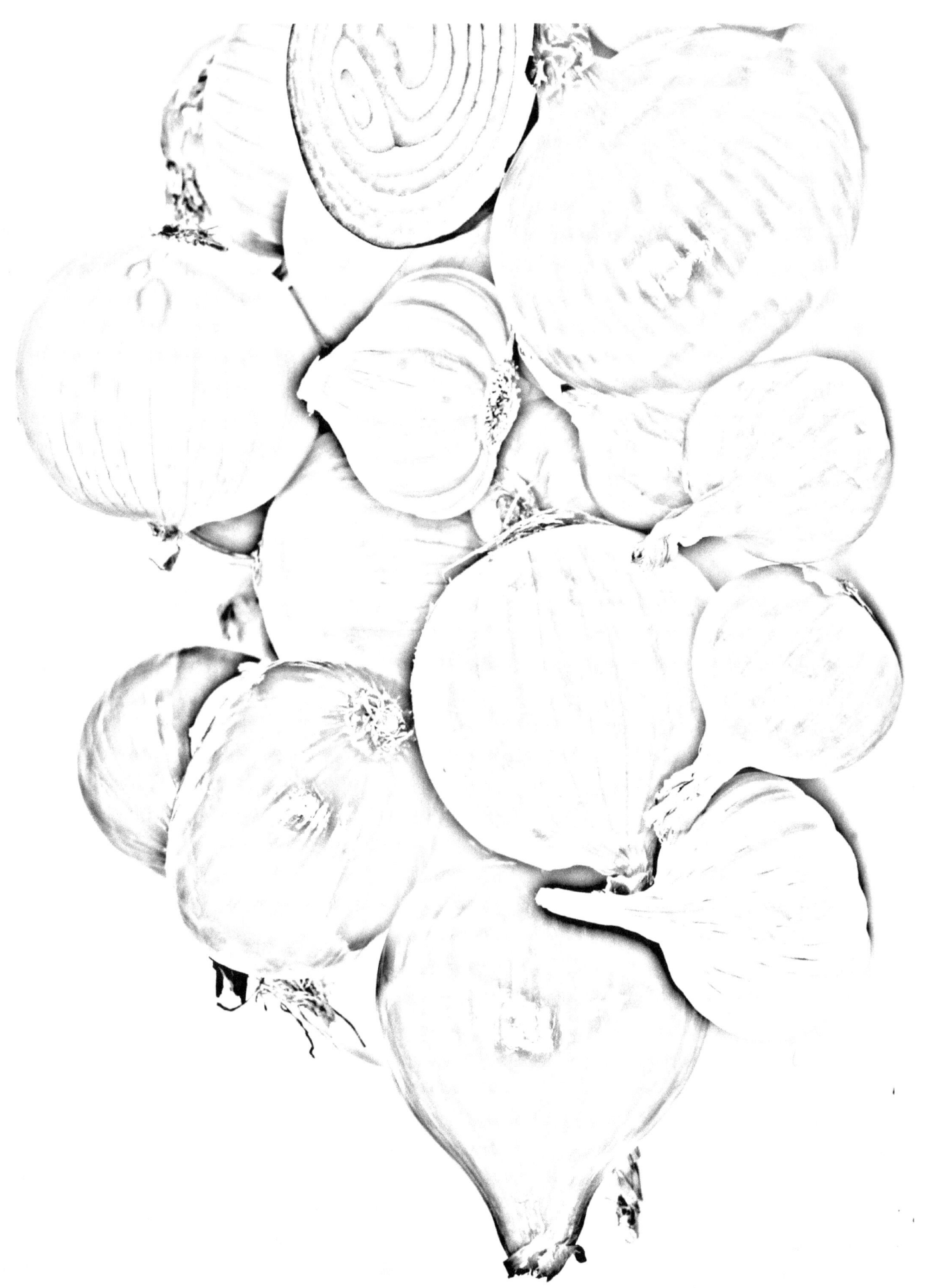

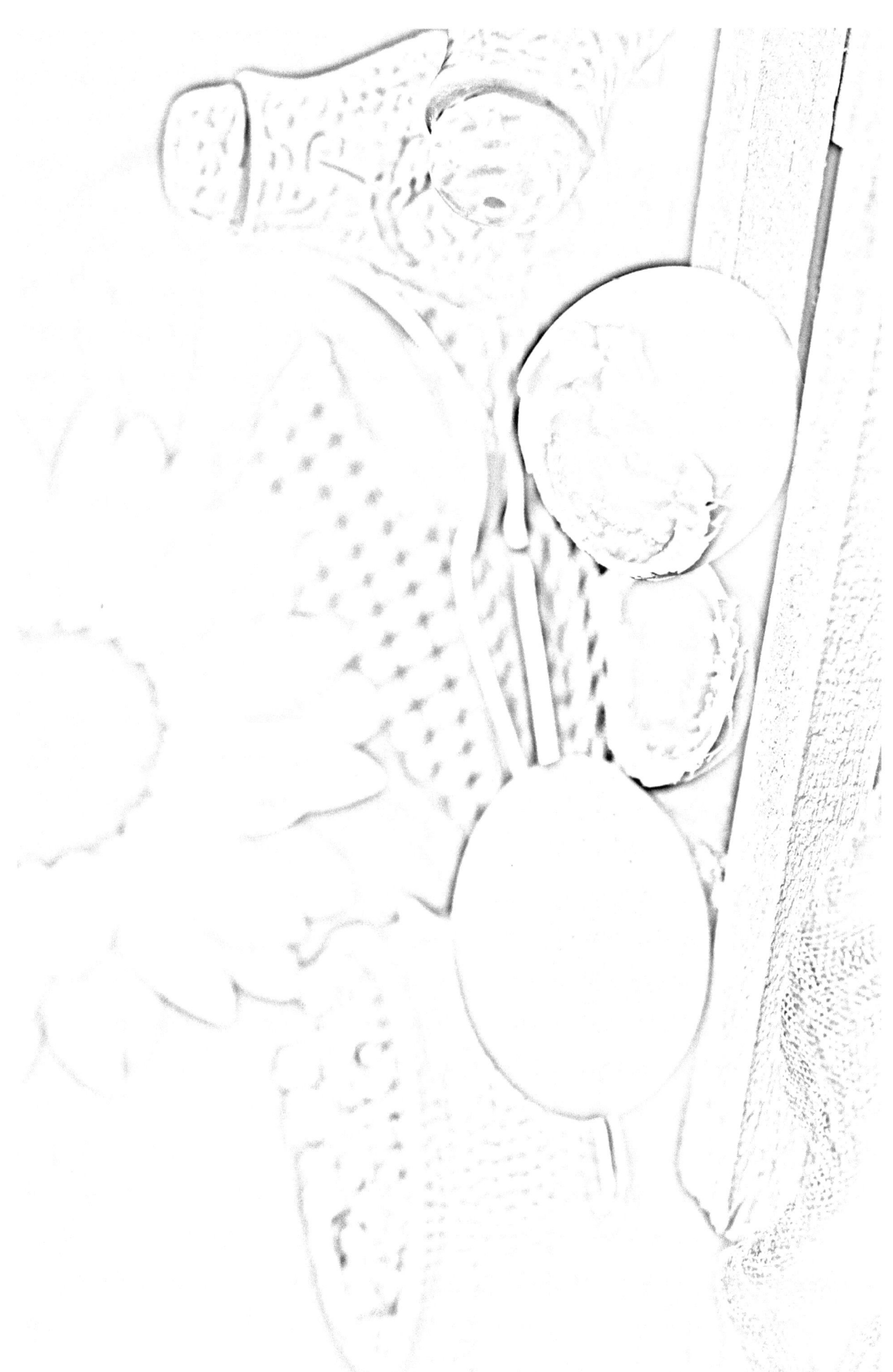

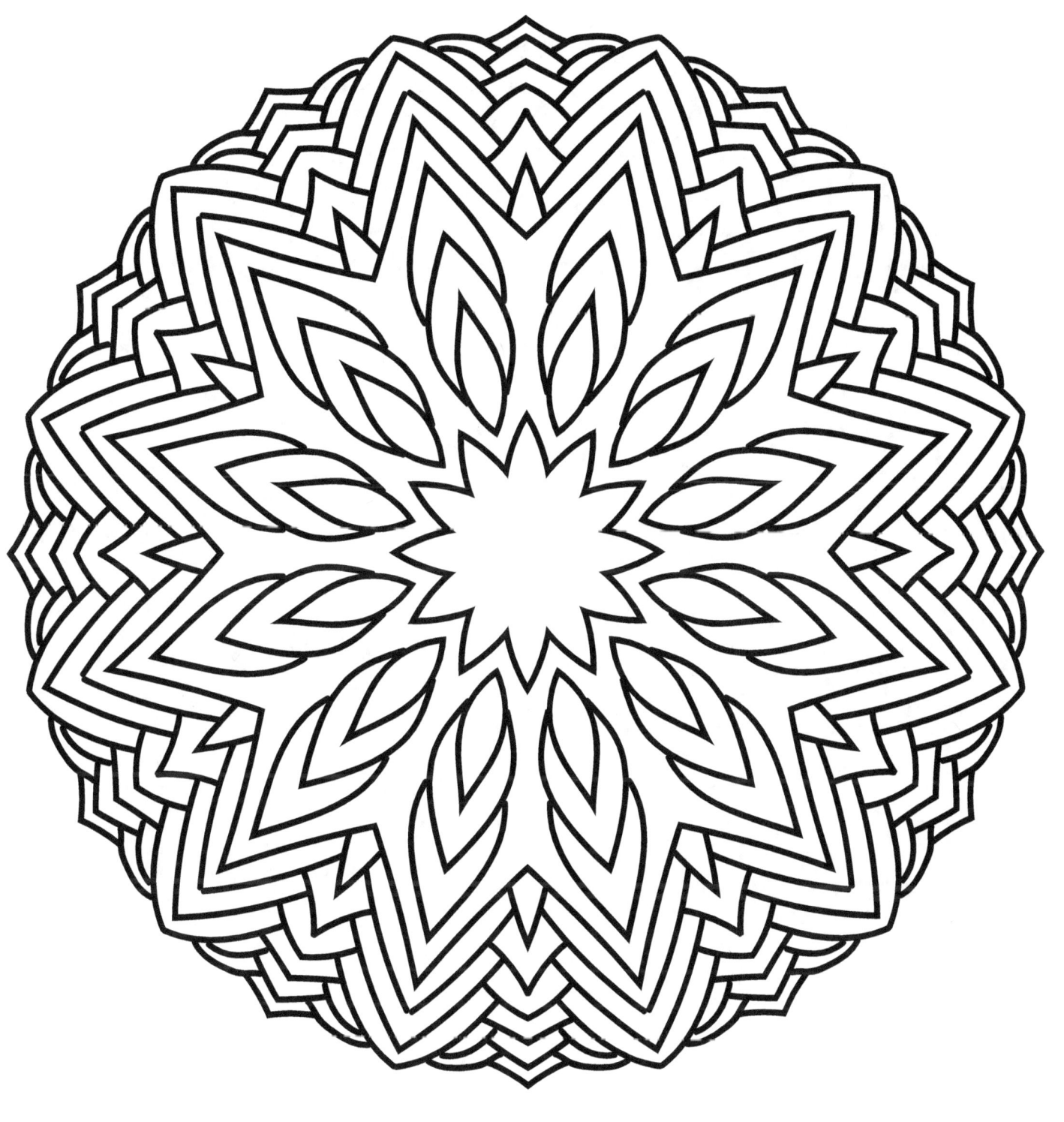

Look for other types of beautiful designs to color by author/illustrator Patricia Markham

(Mandala designs are featured in The Commuting Colorist Series - Books 1-5)

www.ingramcontent.com/pod-product-compliance
Lightning Source LLC
Chambersburg PA
CBHW062121220526
45471CB00010B/3830